HUMAN (and) ANIMAL
INTERRELATIONSHIPS

From Domestication to Present

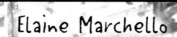

Elaine Marchello

Kendall Hunt
publishing company

Cover image credits:
Chicago Stockyards © Underwood & Underwood/CORBIS
Cheetah and Carving © Jupiterimages Corporation
Building and Cave Painting © Shutterstock, Inc. Used under license.

Kendall Hunt
publishing company

www.kendallhunt.com
Send all inquiries to:
4050 Westmark Drive
Dubuque, IA 52004-1840

Copyright © 2010 by Elaine Marchello

ISBN 978-0-7575-8218-9

Printed in the United States of America
10 9 8 7 6 5 4 3 2

Contents

Chapter 1: Introduction   1

Chapter 2: Domestication   11

Chapter 3: Man as Agriculturalist—Rivers   23 ⌉ 08/31 – 09/07

Chapter 4: Man as Agriculturalist—Traders   39

Chapter 5: Ancient Animals—Real or Not Real?   49

Chapter 6: Man as Agriculturalist—Feudal   61 ⌉ → 09/12.

Chapter 7: Man as Agriculturalist—Colonial   75

Chapter 8: Pioneer   83

Chapter 9: Empire (United States)   91

Chapter 10: Man as the Industrialist—Britain   99

Chapter 11: Man as the Industrialist—Purebred   105

Chapter 12: Man as a Scientist (Informationalist)   115

Chapter 13: Exotic Animals and the History of Zoos   121

Chapter 14: Animism and Totemism   133

Chapter 15: Animals in Mythology, Art, Literature, and Screen   145

Chapter 16: History of How Animal Ethics Developed   161

✓ **Chapter 17:** Experimenting with Humans and Animals: A Brief History   173 ⌉ 11/30

1 Introduction

Objectives

○ To learn how the early philosophers viewed humans and animals

○ To learn about the natural philosophers during Medieval and Renaissance times

○ To be introduced to various creation myths and some of the theories of evolution

○ To establish a timeline and classify man and his relationships with animals into four main categories: hunter, agriculturalist, industrialist, and scientist

Introduction

- Over 200 different dog breeds
- Cows of 20,000 years ago probably produced barely enough milk for her calf; today's Holstein produces 20,000 pounds of milk per lactation
- Man and livestock came together during domestication; probably because we have to consider that man is, himself, an animal
- *1 million animal species, only 33 have been domesticated.*

Some things to think about.....

- Africa is still sometimes troubled by outbreaks of the leopard men, who disguise themselves as leopards with masks and metal claws, pounce on a victim who they kill by piercing the jugular with their claws, and then eating part of their body
- India: sacred cows wander streets unmolested
- Egyptian mob murdered a Roman for killing a cat
- Early Christians were accused of worshipping a donkey
- Norse berserkers in the skins of bears or wolves were feared for their crazed ferocity in battle
- Finn (who we will learn about later) could turn into a deer or dog at will
- Some animals are said to sense the presence of ghosts
- It is lucky to see a white horse
- A black cat can be either a good luck charm or an omen of evil
- The devil frequently appeared in animal form to witches

History of Evolutionary Thought

The Great Chain of Being
• God
↓
• angels
↓
• Demons
↓
• man
↓
• animals
↓
• plants
↓
• minerals
↓
• non being

Greek

- Xenophanes (576–480 BC)
  1st person to have recognized that fossils were remnants of organisms

- Aristotle (384–322 BC)
  vitalist. Believed that living things were animated by a vital force different from anything found in nonliving matter.

  Believed that living things were animated by a vital force different from anything found in nonliving matter
  The Great Chain of Being

Roman

- Lucretius (99–55 BC)
  Rejected most of Aristotles work

  Summed up much of the non-Aristotelian Greek thoughts in a work called De Rerum Natura (On the Nature of Things)
  A poem of six books *LoL*
  Goal was to explain Epicurean philosophy to a Roman audience

- Pliny (23–79 AC)
Recorded what was then known about nature and natural processes in a monumental and influential book
Problem: *much misinformation was included*

Decline of Science

was ∅ caused by the rise in Christianity. Seemed to be preoccupied with myth and spirituality

Seemed to be a preoccupation with myth and spirituality

Middle Ages

All scholarly activity was centered in the church, and it is not surprising that science continued to be neglected

Early Theologians

- Augustine (354–430) and Thomas Aquinas (1225–1275)
Suggested a naturalistic interpretation patterned after Aristotle

THO: AQVINVS

© 2010, Jupiter Images Corporation

   These interpretations were denounced in the thirteenth century
      Diversity of opinion was considered as heresy
      Free discussion carried with it the risk of reprimand and excommunication
- Augustine
Believed that the events in the Bible should not be interpreted literally if it contradicts what we know from science and our God-given reason.

- Thomas Aquinas
Empirist = uses experience to gain knowledge, not experimentation

   Denied that human beings have any duty of charity to animals because they are not persons; otherwise it would be unlawful to use them for food
   BUT, this reasoning does NOT give license to be cruel to animals because that might carry over to human beings

The Renaissance

Fifteenth and sixteenth centuries during the revival of Greek and Roman art and learning did not extend much to natural history

New discoveries were made in anatomy and physiology (Da Vinci), but not in evolution

The Natural Philosophers

Seventeenth and eighteenth centuries were notable for conceptual, primarily descriptive works of a group of scholars who made some advances in evolutionary thought

- Francis Bacon (1561–1626)
  Urged abandonment of Aristotelian philosophy and instead rely on experiment, observation and inductive reasoning *He suggested that variations in nature were important and indicated that change was possible in species.*

- René Descartes (1596–1650)
  Wrote about the possibility of changes in the universe (and species by implication)
  His writings were not published until after his death to avoid offending the church
- Carl Linnaeus (1707–1778)
  Developed the modern system of biological nomenclature (species, genus, etc.)

- John Ray (1627–1705)
  First to clearly define the species concept in terms of ancestry and interfertility (although he did not speculate on evolution)
- de Maupertuis (1698–1759)
  Known primarily as an astronomer and mathematician
  Developed many modern concepts in embryology, genetics, and evolution
  Suggested that species could change based on mutation, selection, and isolation.

- Georges-Louis Leclerc, Comte de Buffon (1707–1788)
  Perhaps the most influential of the eighteenth-century natural philosophers
  Wrote extensively
  Hedged on evolution, but was stimulus to later thinking about it
- Desiderius Erasmus, Charles Darwin, and Jean-Baptiste Lamarck
  Each discussed the evidence for evolution and proposed similar processes to account for it
  This process has come to be called inheritance of acquired characteristics, according to which changes caused to organisms by the environment were thought to be transmissible to offspring.

Creation Myths

(of which there are many!)
- Etiological
  Concerns the beginnings of things and stem from primitive speculation about their origin

- Ritual
  Connected with various periodic ceremonies, particularly at the New Year, designed to ensure the continuation and well-being of the state or even the world

Birth of Earth & Sky
Egypt

- Pyramid texts written by Heliopolis (2480–2137 BC)
  Talked about the god, Atum, a mysterious deity who was often associated with the sun god Re
  Heliopolis believed there had been a primordial waste of water called Nun
  Atum began creation from this Nun; but he needed firm ground to work on—this was the primordial hill where creation of the world began and is the site of Atum's temple at Heliopolis

Sumer: Enke

- Enke, the god associated with fresh waters, figures most as the creator in early Sumerian texts
  Enke arrives by sea and impregnates Ninhursag, the mother of the land
  This fertilizing produces plants and necessary food
  He also invents the pick axe and brick mould, the essential implements of Mesopotamia economy
  Enke goes further + causes humans to be fashioned out of clay to act as servants so the gods did not have to toil.

Sumer: Marduk

- Most famous creation myth is the Babylonian *Enuma elish*
  Tiamat was a great monster that the god Marduk slays
  The god Marduk creates heaven + earth from her body

Genesis

- The Bible and the book of Genesis
  God creates the world in six days and rests on the seventh
  Also the story of Adam and Eve follow along

Evolution

10–20 billion years ago—the universe began

- Big Bang Theory

For several hundred thousand years immediately after that, the universe was too hot for elements to form, so it consisted of a mix of subatomic particles and radiation

As universe cooled, the first hydrogen and helium atoms began to form.

5 billion years ago-sun and planets formed

- First 2 billion years, one continent, Pangaea, broke up and formed the continental configuration of today.

  At the dawn of the Paleozoic era, Gondwanaland (land mass) was formed late in the Precambrian era. It sat in what is now the South Pacific and extended as far down as the South Pole.

  On the opposite side of the globe, Laurentia, a small continent, sat straddling the Equator and later grew to become North America.

  Baltica, now most of Europe, lay to the east of Laurentia.

  Various other continental masses, most now form sections of Asia, were scattered in places as yet unknown to us.

Second 3 billion years—life was initiated

- Biological populations evolved by natural selection "survival of the fittest"

  50 million years ago: Age of mammals began

  25 million years ago: Climate cooled; extensive grasslands appeared.

  20 million years ago: common ancestors of man and other primates appeared

Evolutionary Timeline DO NOT NEED TO MEMORIZE

Life Forms	Millions of years Ago	Period	Era
Humans	0	Quaternary	Cenozoic
Mammals arrive	50	Tertiary	
Dinosaurs flourish, tyrannosaurus rex, triceratops, etc.	100	Cretaceous	Mesozoic
Reptiles, pre-bird, archaeopteryx	150–175	Jurassic	
Proliferation of land plant life	200	Triassic	

Reptile branches, pre-mammalian form. Dinosaurs arrive	250	Permian	Paleozoic
Amphibians and first reptiles on land	300	Carboniferous	
Plants from the sea began to colonize the land	350	Devonian	
Vertebrate fish, jawless	425	Silurian	
Marine invertebrates, trilobites, cephalopods	450–500	Ordovician	
Trilobites, snails, brachipods	500–575	Cambrian	
Multicellular life forms, soft-bodied animals, worms, jellyfish, etc.	600–650	Algonkian	Precambrian
Life begins 3.5 billion years ago			

Thank god . . .

Theories of Evolution

1800s three individuals proposed explanations for biological evolution

- Jean Baptiste Lamarck (1744–1829)
- Charles Darwin (1809–1882)
- Alfred Russel Wallace (1823–1913)

Jean Baptiste Lamarck

Environment affects the shape + organization of animals

Frequent use of any organ, when confirmed by habit, increases the function of that organ.

Giraffe example *He believed that the long necks of giraffes evolved as generations of giraffes reached higher.*

Alfred Russel Wallace

Struggle for existence. Weakest + least perfectly organized must always succumb. Came to almost the same conclusion as Darwin.

Came to almost the same conclusion as Darwin, which Darwin acknowledged

Charles Darwin, Naturalist

H.M.S. Beagle (5 years)
Natural Selection
"Convinced that species are not immutable, but that those belonging to what are called the same genera are lineal descendents of some other and generally extinct species, in the same manner as the acknowledged varieties of any one species are the descendents of that species." Taken from Darwin's abstract on his Theory of Natural Selection.

From evolution to….

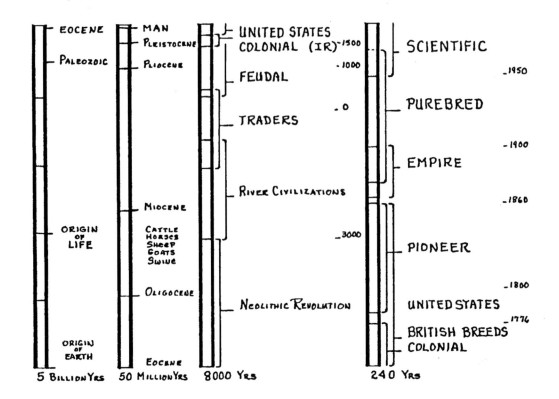

5 BILLION YRS	50 MILLION YRS	8000 YRS	240 YRS

EOCENE
PALEOZOIC
ORIGIN OF LIFE
ORIGIN OF EARTH

MAN
PLEISTOCENE
PLIOCENE
MIOCENE
CATTLE
HORSES
SHEEP
GOATS
SWINE
OLIGOCENE
EOCENE

UNITED STATES
COLONIAL (IR) -1500
-1000
FEUDAL
-0
TRADERS
RIVER CIVILIZATIONS
-3000
NEOLITHIC REVOLUTION

SCIENTIFIC
-1950
PUREBRED
-1900
EMPIRE
-1860
PIONEER
-1800
UNITED STATES
-1776
BRITISH BREEDS
COLONIAL

Man and his interrelationship with animals can be broken down into four classifications

- Hunter
- Agriculturalist
- Industrialist
- Informationalist (scientist)

Study Questions

1. The Big Bang Theory was
   a. The theory of how the Beatles got started
   b. The theory of how the extinction of dinosaurs came about
   c. The theory of how the matter and energy in our universe came to be
   d. The theory that was used to invent gun powder

2. Of the 1 million animal species in the world, only about __33__ have been domesticated.
   a. 23
   b. 33
   c. 43
   d. 53

3. About 5 billion years ago, one continent, __Pangaea__ broke up and formed the continental configuration of today.
   a. Gondwanaland
   b. Laurentia
   c. Pangaea
   d. Baltica

4. Who was the first person to have recognized that fossils were remnants of organisms?
   a. Xenophanes
   b. Aristotle
   c. Lucretius
   d. Pliny

5. Which Greek philosopher created the Great Chain of Being?
   a. Xenophanes
   b. Aristotle
   c. Lucretius
   d. Pliny

6. Who urged abandonment of Aristotle's philosophy and said we should rely on experiment?
   a. Bacon
   b. Descartes
   c. Linnaeus
   d. Ray

7. Which of the early philosophers, who was known as an astronomer and mathematician, suggested that species could change based on mutation, selection, and isolation?

    a. Aristotle

    c. de Maupertuis

    b. Ray

    d. Comte de Buffon

8. Which of the following is NOT one of the classifications of man and his interrelationships with animals?

    a. Hunter

    b. Agriculturalist

    c. Consumerist

    d. Industrialist

2 Domestication

Objectives

- ❍ To learn how man developed and became omnivores
- ❍ To learn some of the theories of where fire came from
- ❍ To see the significance of cave art
- ❍ To define humanities
- ❍ To define domestication and use the canine timeline as an example
- ❍ To see how animals were being used by the developing people

Hunter

10 million BC	Hominoids developed
2 million BC	Man became omnivorous
500,000 BC	Man began to control fire
300,000 BC	*Homo sapiens* developed
20,000 BC	Cave art
10,000 BC	Last glacial retreat
8,000 BC	Domestication of animals and plants
7,000 BC	Walled city of Jericho
5,000 BC	Summer culture developed
4,000 BC	Egyptian culture began

- Meat: most important

- Cut down harvest time and bulk consumption by two-thirds
  - Met salt requirement

- Allowed more time for man to interact socially and develop early communication skills

How Man Started

- *Homo habilis*
  2 million years ago
  Dominant hominoid
  used chipped stone tools
  Omnivorous

- *Homo erectus*
  Spread over Eurasia and Africa (during Pleistocene epoch)
  Ran erect
  Used a spear
  Made flacked tools + weapons
  Hunted in packs of 40, Killed large animals.

- Animals
  - Bison hunted the most. used all parts of the animal.

- Fire

- *Homo Erectus* discovered fire
  Warmth
  Predator control
  Hunting tool
  Maintaining desirable plant communities
  Cooking
  Fire as a substitute for food: can replace energy lost through cold exposure

Origin of Fire

Many legends or myths relating to the origin of fire

- Stealing fire from the gods
Prometheus—stole fire from Zeus and gave it to the mortals; in return, Zeus created Pandora

- Apache Indian tale
Fox stole fire from the fireflies and spread it with his tail

Celtic

- Finn held fire to be the child of the sun that descended from the heavens where it was rocked in a tub of yellow copper

European folklore

- Some Indians of Brazil believe the stolen flame was hidden among the trees, because fire could be found readymade in the smoldering of a lightening-charred tree
- Fire was also produced by rubbing two pieces of wood together
Oak, a hard wood, was great for fire making and was considered sacred
- Mistletoe, which grows on oak, became a protective charm against lightning
An acorn carried in the pocket gave security to the traveler

As time went on...

Hunt created need to spread out and migrate with the herds

Man moved from individual scavenger to member of food-gathering and hunting society

300,000 years ago, *Homo sapiens* appeared

- "Neanderthal" man (60,000 years ago)

- Buried dead with ceremony and developed beliefs concerning the supernatural.

"Gnawed bones around the campfire"

- We still have visions of this even though most diets now are cereal based
- Bones around the campfire are still associated with all masculine strength and passion which is further perpetuated through myths and most cultures
Example: yeomen of Norman lords were given extra rations of beef to cement their loyalty and were dubbed "beefeaters"

Shakespeare

- Shakespeare's Henry V speaks of beef on the eve of the Battle of Agincourt: "…and then give them great meals of beef and iron and steel, they will eat like wolves and fight like devils"
- Today: still follow ritual of broiling red meat over a charcoal grill and devouring it with symbolic relish

Symbols and Language

50,000–40,000 years ago *Cro-magnon* man replaced Neanderthal

- Developed symbolic language skills
- Diversified cultures
- Followed a single animal species over its range

© 2010, Jupiter Images Corporation

20,000 years ago

- People left mark on environment
- Represent humanities beginnings
- Many cave paintings feature the majestic bull

Cave Paintings

Works of art that capture the essence of movement familiar only to those who have studied the animals in detail

- Cave art signaled the technology of man; raising from ill-equipped mammal in an ecosystem to a shaper of his environment

© 2010, Jupiter Images Corporation

Major Caves

Altamira
Lascaux
Chauvet
Northern Africa Saharan rock art

Altamira

- Northern Spain (16,000–19,000 BC)

Paintings primarily focus on bison

- Also have horses, deer, wild boar portrayed; all animals, no landscape
- Used paints derived from natural earth pigments like ochre and zinc oxides
- Used multiple colors; Used facets of rocks to complement the animal design
- Discovered more advanced lighting approaches

Lascaux
- Discovered in 1940 by four teenagers and a dog
- Open to public after World War II, but carbon dioxide started damaging the walls so it closed to public in 1963
- In 1983, opened up a replica cave
  2,188 animal figures in 110 different caves
- Very large and artifacts were better preserved
- Bulls, bison, horses; also some human signs
- Animal art was more defined
- These caves were not dwellings

{virtual walking tour}

Chauvet
- Discovered in 1994 (30,000 BC) (wrong?)
  Although there is some question as to the date of the cave
- Fourteen different animal species depicted
  Horses, lions, rhinos, mammoths, bears, bison, ibex, reindeer, red deer, aurochs, megaceros deer, musk-oxen, panther, owl
- Two parts of cave
  1st: Images are red with black/engraved

  2nd: part of animals are mostly black

Northern Africa Saharan Rock Art
Three periods
- Bubalus
- Cattle
- Horse

Bubalus
- End of sixth to mid fourth millennium BC
- Art shows animals that became extinct in that area (buffalo, elephant, rhino, hippo)

Cattle
- Mid-fourth to mid-second millennium BC
- No longer displayed buffalo

- Some other wild animals
- Mainly cattle
- Animals are less natural and sketchier
- Shows herdsmen

© 2010, Jupiter Images Corporation

Horse
- From ca. 1200 BC
- Three subperiods
  - chariot
  - Horsemen
  - Horse + camel

Included other animals such as antelope oryx, gazelles, moufflons, ostrich, zebu, and goats

Hunting and Gathering

10,000 BC
Hunting and gathering societies had colonized most of the world
More of the world became available as the ice sheets receded
around 7,000 BC West Asia + Egypt people begin keeping domesticated animals (sheep.)
- Wall of Jericho
  Jericho was the oldest walled town in the world
  Somewhere around 7000 BC
  Farmed as well as hunted
  - May have irrigated crops

  According to the Bible, the walls came tumbling down
  Israelites fleeing from Egypt destroyed the ancient city under mysterious circumstances

- Catal Huyuk, 8000 BC
  Area now called Turkey
  Prospered for more than 2000 years
  Abandoned around 5600 BC for unknown reasons
  Site found in 1961
  Tools, wall paintings, etc.
  Raised goats and sheep
  Had ⌀ doors; used a ladder + a hole in the roof.

Moving on....

9,000 BC

- Made first domestication: Asiatic wolf (actually may have been domesticated as early as 15,000 BC)
- Became known as the dog
  Wolf was carnivorous competitor of man; provided his acute senses to hunt and in return, man provided a share of kill and love

Canine Timeline

1 million BC
  The gray wolf family becomes the world's largest canine group.

100,000 BC
  Gray wolves and subspecies are spread across Asia, the Middle East, Europe and America. Man begins selecting wolves for puppy characteristics as camp pets.

20,000–10,000 BC
  Stone Age man breeds dogs for his own purposes. Oldest evidence is 14,000 year-old jaw with teeth of modern dog found in Iraq.

7000 BC
  Egyptians develop dogs from their region, Tibet and China.

4500 BC
  Fossils of the period are of pointer types, mastiffs, greyhounds, shepherds and the wolf-like spitz.

3500 BC
  Basic dog types reach Europe.

3000 BC
  Prototype pointer skeleton found in England exhibits evidence of greyhound and mastiff characteristics. Modern hunting dogs will evolve from these, called *Canis familiaris intermedius.*

2000 BC
  As the Neolithic period ends, most basic breeds are established.

23–79 AD
  The Roman Pliny writes about hunters carrying dogs that stiffen and point their noses at game concealed in undergrowth.

100–1500 AD
  Though there are few breeds in any one region, breeds and strains number into the thousands worldwide.

1800-1900 AD
  Distinctive breed separations and refinements advance rapidly through kennel clubs and knowledge of scientific animal breeding. About 400 breeds exist today.

© 2010, Jupiter Images Corporation

© Iantapix, 2010. Used under license from Shutterstock, Inc.

Glacier Retreat

- Some clans followed herds of cloven-hoofed animals and developed a nomadic way of life
  - reindeer
  - sheep / goat
- 10,000 years ago, during the glaciations, areas south of the ice were ideal for game and edible plants (ex: Sahara desert was a savanna)
- References to the Garden of Eden may go back to this time, because of plentiful food supply
- As glacial retreat was followed by warm, dry weather, many plant and animal species perished because of climatic change

- Helped develop the herdsman
  - Famine stalked human clans
  - Developed agriculture
  - Domestication of plants and animals for food.

Neolithic Revolution Began, 8000–6000 BC

- Climatic shifts from the end of the Ice Age prompted migration of big game animals to new pasture lands in Northern areas
- Also changed growth patterns of many plants
- Human population increased
  - Forced humans to band together to hunt + plant

During this time….

- Wolves were domesticated; used to track and corner game

- Sheep, goats, and pigs were first domesticated in the Middle East between 8500–7000 BC
- Horned cattle (6500 BC)
  Domestication may have been originally motivated by religious sentiments rather than for food and clothing

Cattle and Sheep

- Hides/wool
  Clothes, containers, shelters, crude boats
- Horns/bones
  Needles and utensils
- Manure
  Enrich soil and improve crop yield

- provided protein-rich meat and milk

Study Questions

1. What did Prometheus steal from the gods?
   a. Salt
   b. Gold
   c. Fire
   d. Ice cream

2. Which of the ancient men was the first to bury their dead with ceremony?
   a. Homo habilis
   b. Homo erectus
   c. Neanderthal man
   d. Cro-magnon man

3. The horse period of Northern Africa Saharan Rock Art had three subperiods. Which of the following is NOT one of those subperiods?
   a. Chariot
   b. Horsemen
   c. Horse and camel
   d. Llama

4. What animal was domesticated to ultimately be what we know now as the dog?
   a. Wolf
   b. Wolverine
   c. Dingo
   d. Chihuahua

5. What was the most important contribution of animals to the cultural evolution of man?
   a. Salt
   b. Bread
   c. Wine
   d. Meat

3

Man as Agriculturalist– Rivers

Objectives

❍ To learn about the four ancient river civilizations and the people and animals that inhabited them

❍ To become aware of some of the history during and after these times and how it affected animals

❍ To learn how man started to use agriculture more frequently and why

❍ Define domestication

❍ To learn where money originated and the associated myth

© 2010, Jupiter Images Corporation

Rivers
Traders
Feudal
Colonial
Pioneer
Rivers

The four river civilizations
- Sumer on the Tigris and Euphrates in Mesopotamia
- Egypt on the Nile
- India on the Indus
- China on the Yellow

Cultures (6000 BC to 600 BC)

Sumer on the Tigris and Euphrates Rivers–culture began

- The rivers were subject to violent floods in the spring; this flood plain had no natural barriers around it, so the history of Mesopotamia is one of continual invasion by developing groups of people who, in time, were absorbed into the agriculture and cultural activities of the settled people.

4000 BC—Sumerian culture flourished

- Region known as the Cradle of Civilization
- Life was affected by two factors
  ○ Unpredictability of Tigris and Euphrates floods
  ○ Richness of river valleys (soil)
- Using fertile land and water…

  ○ Could pass agricultural techniques to others

3700 BC
- Invented the wheel
- First plow

- Women had a high place in society
- Banking originated

- Ancient Sumeria: worshipped the bull god Enlil as the god of storm and supreme god of fertility
- Mesopotamia is the suspected spot of the "Garden of Eden"

After Sumer came

- Babylonians
- Hittites with iron weapons and horses
- Assyrians
- Chaldeans
- Then the Medes and Persians who formed a massive empire that covered most of the Near East and stretched toward India

Egypt on the Nile River

- 5500 BC evidence of organized, permanent settlements focused on agriculture
- Hunting was no longer primary source of food
- Egyptian diet was made up of domesticated cattle, sheep, pigs, and goats as well as cereal grains

Animals of Ancient Egypt

- Domesticated sheep, cattle, goats, pigs, geese, and later horses

Supplied

- Milk, wool, meat, eggs, leather, skins, horns, fat, and manual labor

Birds of Ancient Egypt

- Falcon, kite, goose, crane, heron, plover, pigeon, ibis, vulture, and owl
- Chickens may have come from Africa
- Falcon

- Ibis
  ○ Sacred, hermit, or glossy

Fish of Ancient Egypt

- Some species were sacred and could not be eaten
- Common were the carp, perch, and catfish

© 2010, Jupiter Images Corporation

© 2010, Jupiter Images Corporation

- The poor ate fish more than meat (more available)
- The pharaohs and priests could not eat fish because certain fish were sacred to SET, one of the gods the pharaohs aligned themselves with

Cattle of Ancient Egypt

- Cow was sacred to many goddesses
- Bulls were sacred to Ra
- Strong connection with solar imagery to the ancient Egyptians
- The ancient, pre-dynastic period cattle themselves were a long-horned variety
- Used for sacrificial purposes as well as for draft purposes
- Later, the cattle became thinner and shorter horned

- The long-horned breed of oxen were fattened, then adorned with ostrich feathers and displayed in processions with their owners before ritual sacrifice to the gods
- During Ramses III reign, 16,000 cattle were sacrificed per year just to one god, Amen
- Interestingly....

Pigs and Goats in Ancient Egypt

- Pork was eaten regularly and not used in Egyptian religion
- Goat meat was eaten by many, even upper class

Also tried to domesticate: hyenas, gazelles, and cranes without much success

- Sheep and goats ("small cattle") were kept for meat, milk, wool, and hide
- Goats

- Pigs were prevalent and were also listed among the assets of various temples

Horses

- Came a bit later and were introduced by the Hyksos
- Donkeys were used for transportation and as pack animals

- Horses were used for ceremonial processions, hunting, and war where they were harnessed to the chariot

- Given as prestige gifts between Egyptians and rulers in north Africa and the Near East
- Height of these horses: 1.35–1.5 meters tall (4.4–4.9 feet tall)

Pets in Ancient Egypt

- Monkeys, ducks, geese, pigeons, hoopoes, falcons, cats, dogs, and ferrets
- Cats were both pets and symbols of cat deities
- Cats often accompanied the master to help with the hunting and fowling

Dogs in Ancient Egypt

- Hunted with the master
- Watch dogs
- Never shown as an animal to be petted
- Types of dogs were related to the basenji, saluki, greyhound, mastiff, and dachshund

Goose in Ancient Egypt

- The Nile goose
- Had a vile temper, but often had the run of the house and garden
- There were sacred lakes that were home to the sacred geese

Other Unusual Pets

- Ramses II had a tame lion
- Sudanese Cheetahs sometimes took the place of house cats

Wildlife the Egyptians Knew About

- Lions, cheetahs, wolves, antelope, wild bulls, hyenas, jackals, snakes, mongoose, and desert hares

- Nile River
  Filled with crocodiles, hypos, turtles, frogs, fish, and birds

Insects

- Bees, sacred beetles, locusts, flies, centipedes, and scorpions
- Bees
  - Were kept for honey and wax
  - Kept in wicker hives covered in clay

© 2010, Jupiter Images Corporation

◦ The honey was used by the Egyptians to create make-up and medicine as well as for food and as offerings to the gods

More Egypt...

- Nile River had predictable floods that left rich deposits of alluvial soil that made wheat growing easy
- After flood, land was resurveyed, plowed, and broadcast with seed that was trampled into the ground by swine

Lower and upper Egypt joined in 3100 BC

- Thirty dynasties of pharaohs ruled Egypt until 332 BC when Alexander the Great conquered
- Because Egypt was protected by natural barriers (Red Sea on east, desert on west) it developed a continuous culture save for one invasion: in 1730 the Hyksos, a Sematic tribe with horses and chariots conquered Egypt

- Egyptians used the horse quite heavily for chariots
- Had 70,000 chariot horses

India on the Indus River

- Goes back to 3000 BC
- Eventually discovered urbanization, metalworking, and writing
- BUT DISAPPEARED!!
- Egypt, Mesopotamia, and the Yellow River civilizations all lasted for millennia and left marks
- Indus civilization was a false start

Harappans

- The Harappans are the people who lived in India at this early time
- Were agricultural people: horticulture

- Wet/marshy environment: rhinoceros, elephants, tigers
- Domesticated: camels, cats, dogs, sheep, goats, buffalo

Disappeared without a trace

- Not much known about how Harappans disappeared
- 1800–1700 BC, no trace of what happened to them
- Cities were covered by soil and lost

Aryans were new start in Indian culture

- Aryans invaded or came in to area and settled in Indus valley
  - poultry were produced
  - cereal crops
- 1500 BC with herds of cattle
- Zebu cattle of India are now thought to be derivations of the same wild cattle from which nonhumped cattle originated
  - Introduced milking
  - Caused India to protect cattle "sacred cow"

China on the Yellow River

-Also known as the Yellow River Valley

© 2010, Jupiter Images Corporation

- Chinese history mixed with fact and legend

- Irrigated millet (4000 BC)
- Yellow River was the site of vast irrigation of millet long before the Shang Dynasty of 1760 BC
  - Silkworm
  - Pig production
    - Household Scavenger
- Later came wet-rice cultivation
- Southern areas
- Domesticated animals early on, but still continued as hunter society as well
- Chinese rulers were obsessed with the horse

Along with the four river civilizations, there were many pastoral societies moving in intricate patterns on the Steppes of Eurasia and Asia
- Scythians were mounted bowmen who followed great herds of stock in these areas
- By 650 BC they raided settled agriculture as far south as Syria and Palestine
- Hoards of horsemen from the steppes of Eurasia were to influence the development of all civilizations until the fourteenth century AD

Between the time of these empires and the Egyptian empire…

- Abraham led tribe out of Ur to Canaan
- While in search of food, went to Egypt
- Became slaves
- Moses led them out of bondage (Red Sea)

Deuteronomy

- Can eat ox, sheep, goat, hart, gazelle, roebuck, wild goat, ibex, antelope, and mountain sheep

  ○ Swine is unclean because it parts the hoof but does not chew the cud.

Timeline: 3000 BC to 560 BC

3000 BC	Herdsmen in Egypt attempted domestication of animals
2700 BC	China—swine household scavengers
2500 BC	Crete—bull prominent in culture; Indus Valley—poultry and cattle
2100 BC	Aryan invasion of India; sacred cow culture started
1730 BC	Hyksos invasion of Egypt; chariot horses brought to culture

Cont…..

1400 BC	Assyria—horses for hunting, cavalry, chariots
1200 BC	Mediterranean Basin-Phoenician horse traders
776 BC	Olympic games; chariot and horse races
753 BC	Rome—Equestrian Order began
650 BC	Settled cultures raided by mounted bowman and pastoralists from steppes
560 BC	Persia—horse-borne communication network

Why agriculture?

- Exactly why man took up agriculture, which requires much effort, in exchange for the seemingly easier life of gathering, herding, and hunting is not fully known
- Possibly due to climatic changes coupled with overpopulation
- Surviving clans probably tried many ways to increase and assure food supply

- Forest agriculture
- Shifting agriculture was tried in many forested areas

• Clear trees by burning, plant crops among stumps and harvet crops until yield goes down (5yrs) then start over in a new area

Near East

- Man succeeded through exotic circumstances
- Genetic accident of wild wheat crossing with goat grass produced Emmer
  - A fertile hybrid with twenty-eight chromosomes; *spread by wind, crosses with another goat grass and produced a larger hybrid with 42 chromosomes called bread wheat.*

Bread Wheat

- Bread wheat will not spread with wind to propagate because ear is too tight
- Man and wheat became symbiotic
- Man figured out how to exploit grain as a principle food
- Store and protect it as well as protecting fields

—supplemental wheat and cereal diets with protein and fat from animal products.

Abraham

- Main source of food for Near East people was wheat and other cereal grains

•Cereals had high carbohydrate but low protein and not enough salt.

- Trade was initiated for salt
- Abraham's story of the Torah epitomizes this change from pastoral nomad to settled agriculturalist
- Pastoral interest in bull and mythology of nomadic life, esp. animal sacrifice of these early cultures of the Fertile Crescent and later the entire Mediterranean Sea

© 2010, Jupiter Images Corporation

Domestication Defined

"Domestication of animals has not only provided a ready supply of food, clothing and companionship, but, in many respects, has changed the way people live and view the world".
(E.O. Price, 2002, Animal Domestication and Behavior).

Domestication

- Sheep and goats (8,000–10,000 years ago)
  - goats ate leafy vegetation; helped clear land
  - sheep furnished wool, meat, fat, and milk

Cattle

- As climate became drier, they were lured to river
- Domestication resulted from this
- Had to be controlled to protect grain fields
  - Castration used on humans was then used on cattle
  - Became versatile providing both power and food.

Swine

- Prolific and excellent scavengers
- Were domesticated separately in Europe and Asia about 9,000 years ago

Ass and onager

- Ass and camel served in caravans
- Onager pulled Chariot in Mesopotamia
- Horse domesticated by pastoralists of the steppes of Eurasia

Llama and alpaca

- Domesticated in South America about 6,000 years ago
- This is about the same time people of the Ukraine began domesticating horses for meat and transportation

Rodents, guinea pigs, and rabbits

- Rodents — exploited for meat and clothing

- Guinea pigs
  Domesticated 3,000–4,000 years ago for food and religious ceremonies
  They arrived in Europe in late sixteenth century AD
- Rabbits
  Domesticated in southern Europe about 2,500 years ago

House mouse

Used for scientific research as early as 1664

- Robert Hooke used a mouse to study the properties of air; Particularly oxygen.

Chickens

Chickens came from jungle fowl

- Cock fighting brought them to Near East from Indus Valley

Wild Turkeys

Domesticated in Europe about 500 years ago

Agriculture

Most powerful invention: Plow

- Yoked oxen to scratch plow
- Meat preservation unknown, therefore consumption had to be immediate
- Ritualization and animal sacrifice
  First to the God to please them
  Later for priests and religions to become more
  powerful

Animal fat: important for cooking and reducing friction.

Wool : used to produce much of the clothing in early civilizations.

- Spinning developed
- Loom was refined later

As development continued.....
- Settlements were along rivers
- Led to irrigation
- Led to cooperation among people
- Development of governments

- Rigid control for forced cooperation led to semi-religious authoritarian monarchs; coupling temporal with religious power made very powerful governments.

and…

- Trade to exchange essential and desired items became common
- Ideas, slaves, and livestock diffused over the known world

- Ass and camel were essential to the lumbering caravans.

Currency

- Currency other than grain or mobile food was invented
- Lydia in Asia Minor, rich in mineral resources developed money
- First western coin was the Lydian Stater which became imperial coinage from 550 BC onward

© 2010, Jupiter Images Corporation

- Sheepskin was used to trap gold in the streams of Lydia; fleeces were dried and burned and the gold lay in the ash.

The Golden Fleece

- Greek myth "Golden Fleece"—sought by Jason and the Argonauts

Beliefs

- Bull was important in Catalhuyuk; cattle were shown as tribute in Sumer
- Egypt: goddess Hathor was represented as a cow and the bull was worshipped at Memphis
- Zodiac: Taurus represents 1/12 of the sky

- Assyrian empire: 5 legged bull with the head of a man stood guard at the gates.

- Babylonia at the gates of Ishtar
- Persian capital at Persepolis has bulls and lions battle in relief
- Greek mythology— The bull was the favorite guise of Zeus.

The list goes on.....

Wars

- Wars of imperial expansion or defense from invaders were common by 3000 BC
- Horse played a singular role

- Mesopotamia people yoked onager to two-wheeled carts or battle wagons
- Horse was yoked to what became the chariot

Problem: onager could pull with its head lowered—did not choke from yoke; horse carried head high and choked down on rough terrain; chariot was only useful on level land (harness and collar comes later)

Study Questions

1. Which ancient river civilization invented the first plow and a math system based on 60?
   a. Sumer
   b. China
   c. India
   d. Egypt

2. Which ancient river civilization was the first to hot-brand cattle?
   a. Sumer
   b. China
   c. India
   d. Egypt

3. What bird of ancient Egypt was the guardian of the ruler?
   a. Falcon
   b. Ibis
   c. Goose
   d. Eagle

4. What meat was eaten regularly in ancient Egypt because it was not used in any religion?
   a. Beef
   b. Pork
   c. Chicken
   d. Emu

5. What animal was often used as an insult during ancient Egyptian times?
   a. Cat
   b. Bird
   c. Pig
   d. Dog

6. What ancient civilization introduced milking of cows?
   a. India
   b. Egypt
   c. China
   d. Sumer

7. What was the genetic accident that led to bread wheat?
   a. Oats
   b. Bermuda
   c. Emmer
   d. Milo

8. As domestication progressed, what animals were prolific and excellent scavengers?
   a. Cats
   b. Ferrets
   c. Swine
   d. Onagers

4 Man as Agriculturalist– Traders

Objectives

○ To learn how man was able to adapt the use of animals for war purposes

○ To see the significance of Ancient Greece and Rome and their respective mythologies

○ To learn how the Roman Coliseum and Circus Maximus were used for entertainment

○ To understand where the mitraic religion comes from and the significance of animals in that religion

Traders

490 BC Greeks, without cavalry, defeated Persians at Marathon
430 BC Greeks became traders after wars decimated agriculture
334 BC Alexander the Great used cavalry in conquest of world
218 BC Hannibal crossed Alps with zebu cattle
214 BC Great Wall of China built to protect Chinese from mounted Mongols
5 BC Birth of Christ
101 AD Mithraic religion spread through Roman Empire; chariot races: Circus Maximus, Coliseum
313 AD Christianity became state religion under Constantine
475 AD Successive waves of Eurasian horsemen ended Roman Empire

- Development of Near East civilization on north and east by pastoralists (who were very restless) was accompanied by settlements starting on the eastern edge of the Mediterranean Sea.

• These seacoast vultures had very limited + frail agricultural resources, therefore trading became essential.

Maritime trading began…
- The Phoenicians on the Levant became the first horse traders
  ○ This started spreading the horse out for use in War
  ○ Their largest colony was in Carthage, North Africa

• Phoenicians developed the alphabet because they wanted to keep written records of transactions.

Greece

- Minoan civilization flourished on Crete in Mediterranean Sea
- 250 BC to 1400 BC—volcanic activity probably ended culture
- Mythology becomes blurred with fact, but cattle worship was part of culture
- The palace in Knossos in the City of King Minos was place of "bull leaping"

Young athletes grasped the horns + vaulted onto the back of a bull and leaped off behind.

- Crete was home of legendary Minotaur: half man, half bull
- The volcanic activity of island sounded like bellows of enraged bulls; which may be reason the Minotaur myth is set in the underground labyrinth of a palace

- o According to the myth, young Greeks were sacrificed to the Minotaur until Theseus slayed it and returned from the labyrinth by the string he had laid while searching for the beast
- Greeks gave human heads to animal bodies; Egyptians earlier gave animal heads to human bodies
- Herding of sheep and goats was a decisive factor in agriculture (until 1000 BC)

Attica grew olive trees and grape vines

- One of the most archaic statues of Greeks is the "Calf Bearer"
- Took 4,000 years to turn the floodplains of Mesopotamia back to desert, but in only 400 years the frail hillsides of Attica were eroded and failed to produce adequate cereal grain.
  This coupled with price fluctuations of the Peloponnesian Wars caused a dependence on trade for cereal.

Destruction of agricultural base made fisherman, sailors, traders, or colonizers out of the Greeks.

- During age of Pericles defined
  - o democratic government
  - o invented philosophy
  - o expressed beauty in humanities (study of people)

Initiated the sciences

- Aristotle became first embryologist. Questions about fetal development.

- Opened incubating hen eggs everyday for twenty-one days to study development

Greek Mythology

often used animals to comment indirectly on human behavior

- Myth of Europa and the bull
  Zeus was a real philanderer. He saw Europa (daughter of King Minos) walking in a pasture by the sea. He turned himself into a white bull. Europa paid him attention and sat on his back.
  He swam to another island and raped her.
  Europe received her name because she was likewise raped by virtually continuous war.

- Poseidon and Athena
  - o These two were arguing over who would be the patron of Athens by giving man his greatest benefit.

Athena won by giving olive tree; Poseidon gave the horse.

- Greek navigation terms were the same as those used in equitation
  - Homer called ships the horses of the sea
  - It has even been suggested that the Trojan Horse was a ship

- Pegasus
  He was caught and broken by Athena (goddess of wisdom). When Billerophon, mortal, set out to kill the chimera, a dragon-like she monster, Athena gave him a golden bridle. He then became the first man to ride and conduct mounted warfare
  This started the romance of dragon slaying—which was revived again in Middle Ages
  Actually, the Sarmations of 300 BC used scale armor made from horses hooves and could have been mistaken for a dragon.

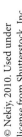

© Nekiy, 2010. Used under license from Shutterstock, Inc.

  - Thrace, the legendary source of the mythological centaur—a creature in which man and horse are one
    - The account in mythology of the battle between the centaurs and the people of Thessaly reflects the fear of settled people for the horsemen
      All the bad + fearsome traits were given to the centaurs by the Greeks.
  - Parthenon frieze of Acropolis in Athens (440 BC) captures the horse in majesty

- Chariot and horse racing went from a religious context to a sport among the Greeks
  - Homer described the chariot race in the games held at Patroclus' funeral
  - Horse racing of 4 miles occurred in 23rd Olympiad of 684 BC
- Before stirrups were invented, horse blocks were maintained along the roadside; horses were taught to kneel
  - Right side mounting was rule: *so can vault on w/ spear in throwing hand.*

- Hippocrates (400 BC) noted swelling in legs of Scythians from constant riding without stirrups

Alexander the Great

- In 339 BC, Philip of Macedonia (country north of Greece) conquered Attica—this began a saga of an empire never repeated
- His son was Alexander the Great
  Tutored by Aristotle

Began military campaigns against Persia, defeating Granicus, Issus, and Arbela
Each time his massed cavalry were important component of the battle
In one battle, *Alex lost Bucephalus, his famous horse*

- Alexander went on the consolidate Greece, Egypt, Persia, and beyond into a vast empire
- Because of Alex's conquests, Hellenism was diffused throughout the western world
- This affected both the Etruscan and Latin cultures of the Italian boot

Rome

- Latins occupied south bank of Tiber
- Palatine hill became stronghold and around it grew the city of Rome from 700 BC on
- Ruling class: *Patricians*

- Plebeians: *peasants + traders*

- Nobles: *who derived power from wealth evolved + replaced Patricians.*

- By 338 BC, Romans gained control of Latin league (city-states of the boot); began saga of empire
  Armies of Rome moved herds of livestock w/ them introduced stock into new area.

- Equestrian Order
  ○ 725 BC, Romulus began the Equestrian Order in the legions (300 mounted men)
  ○ They wore red tunics with two narrow purple stripes
  ○ "Being in the purple" was a sought after honor and may be connected with purple being used for grand and reserve grand champion in stock shows today

City of Rome had 1 million people
- Commanded trade
- Local cereal production insufficient
- Depended on ships from the grain-producing areas of North Africa
  Turned more livestock production
    – sheep, swine, poultry were raised

- Entertainment
  Circus Maximus and Coliseum
  Chariot races
  gladiators fought each other and animals

© 2010, Jupiter Images Corporation

Period of Peace
- 27 BC to 180 AD called the Pax Romana
- Food was fried due to lack of fuel

- Spices from India, especially pepper

  At spice trade height, Romans were spending $25 million a year on spices.

- Silk was another product in great demand from China

http://youtube.com/watch?v=La70eVImTeU& feature=related
= Ben-Hur

Coliseum

- Amphitheatrum Flavium
  ○ Built by the Favain emperors in first century AD as a gift to the Roman citizens
  ○ The emperor Caligula started it, Claudius and Nero ceased work on it, but Vespasian and his son Titus got it finished

In the amphitheatre…

- Venationes (hunts) and munera (gladiatorial games)
  Remained in service for 4 ½ centuries (hunted criminals mostly.)

  The death penalty was being mauled to death by ferocious beasts
  — The condemned person was generally tied to a pole + exposed to the beasts.

- The Hunts
  ○ Initially, the staged hunts were in the morning prior to the gladiator games
  ○ Later, they took place in the afternoon, sometimes lasting for days
  ○ Elephants, bears, bulls, lions, and tigers were captured from all over and brought to the coliseum for these hunts
  Thousands of animals were killed

  ○ At first, the animals were chained
  ○ After providing protection to the audience, the animals were freed
- Venatores, (slaves, criminals, or people under contract) were trained to hunt and kill these animals

As time went on…
Many times, the animals hunted were not killed and could perform other roles

- Tigers – let themselves be kissed

- Lions – catch hares + bring them back unharmed

- Elephants – Tricks like dancing or walking a rope.

- Naval battles
  - Many experts believe that the coliseum could be flooded (through aquaducts)
  - This then allowed mock naval battles to be staged
  - The actors were generally criminals already condemned to death

- During this Roman life
  - Large percentage of people farmed
  - Wheat, olives, grapes, citrus fruits

Cattle were plow power

Sheep + goats grazed/cleaned hillsides

Large estates and villas were granted to the soldiers who had served their empire well
Many officials retired to run estates and many wrote on agriculture in their old age
Ancient literature on Roman farm management is voluminous

Romans were aware of sire input to offspring.

The Bull and Religion

The bull was deeply involved in numerous religions, including
Mithraic (was in direct competition with Christianity)

was considered "Warrior's Religion."

Derived from an old ~~Person~~ Persian Myth:

© Ariy, 2010. Used under license from Shutterstock, Inc.

Mithra was a god of the Persian pantheon; a redeemer god that sat in final judgment (myth resembles Christ).

This god-like athlete lived in a cave and performed many miracles.

In drought, he shot arrows into rocks to obtain water for the people and the stock

Mithra and the White Bull.

While walking one day, Mithra saw a magnificent white bull. He captured him and took him to his cave. They became friends. The supreme sun god, Sol, ordered Mithra to sacrifice the bull. He slit his throat and all useful plants sprang from the bull's body. This was the primordial fertility rite. Wheat sprouted from the bull's spinal column and blood turned to wine; semen was purified by the moon and created all useful animals. By this sacrifice, Mithra had given new life to the world Mithra ascended into heaven in a chariot and cares for those who serve him. In the second coming, he will slay the divine bull and mingle his fat with wine to give his followers immortality.

This religion came to Rome in 67 BC and its following peaked in 308 AD under Emperor Diocletian. It disappeared in 392 AD when Constantine declared Christianity to be the state religion.

Mithraic followers were all men ∅ women.

underground temples abounded around Roman army camps

Caves were called Mithraeums and always contained a Mithraic statue, running water, and long side benches to seat fifty.

Baptized in blood of a bull.

- Statue
  - Mithra is cutting the throat of the white bull; wheat is coming out of the tail and a scorpion attached to the testicles; a snake is going up the shoulder of the bull and a dog is ready to lick the blood from the slit throat

  * Picture of ↑ online.

- Roman empire is decaying from within, hastened by the domino effect created by drought and hardship on Eurasia and the Steppes
- Horsemen
  Many Romans became mounted in the hope of stemming tide of mounted barbarians
  410 AD Rome was sacked by mounted men—Barbarians that destroyed all symbols of Pagan worship
  435 AD European barbarians and Romans were living in sort of harmony

Attila the Hun upset this harmony

Finally stopped by united Europe in northern France
But Eastern Roman empire survived the steppe horsemen and developed into the stoic Byzantine empire under the Rule of the Constantine emperors and Justinian

Attila the Hun upset harmony
  - used stirrups which increased skill
  - Finally stopped by united Europe in N. France.

Study Questions

1. What mythological animal was given all the bad and fearsome traits of man?
   a. Pegasus
   (b.) Centaur
   c. Dragon
   d. Phoenix

2. Who conquered Greece, Egypt, Persia, and more into a vast empire?
   a. Albert the Mighty
   b. Darth Vader ← _LOL what?_
   c. Alexander the Tall
   (d.) Alexander the Great

3. In Rome, who derived power from wealth?
   a. Patricians
   b. Plebians
   (c.) Nobles
   d. Slaves

4. What color was sought after as an honor by the Equestrian order in Rome?
   (a.) Purple
   b. Blue
   c. Red
   d. Green

5. In the coliseum, the men (slaves, criminals, etc.) who hunted were called
   (a.) Venatores
   b. Venetians
   c. Gladiators
   d. Toreadors

6. What ancient group were the first to become aware of and document the sire input in the off-spring?
   a. Greeks
   b. Sumerians
   (c.) Romans
   d. French

7. The Mithraic religion was considered the
   a. Slave's religion
   b. Warrior's religion
   c. Plebian's religion
   d. Co-ed religion

8. According to Mithraic custom, a secret ritual for baptism involved
   a. Horse blood
   b. Moose blood
   c. Bull blood
   d. Sheep blood

5 Ancient Animals– Real or Not Real?

Objectives

○ To become familiar with the ancient myths surrounding ancient animals

○ To learn the importance or significance of the ancient animals studied

○ Become exposed to the history of the study of ancient animals and the people involved

○ To see how ancient animals are still used today in modern-day activities and celebrations

2nd millennium BC

Babylonian epic of creation: Tiamat
A mother goddess (she-dragon) gives birth to brood of monsters who slay her

The god Marduk creates heaven + earth from her body.

Scaly body, serpent's head, viper's horns, front feet of a feline, back ft. of a bird, and tail of

The Phoenix Myths *a scorpion.*

Although, it's a common legend among many ancient civilizations, the origin of the Phoenix myth is attributed to the Egyptians. *(A civilization that was obsessed with eternal life.)*

Phoenix arabica

- Sets its nest of cinnamon twigs on fire, using the flames as a "bath" to cleanse its golden-red plumage of parasites
- 4 feet long, 2 feet high
- Color: golden red with orange eyes
- Food: *eats no meat; likes forest fruits and loves dates.*

Phoenix is the Greek name given to a mythological bird offered in sacrifice to Ra, god of the Sun in ancient Egypt.

- This bird was similar to an eagle and possessed a splendid golden-red plumage that made it look like it was wrapped in flames.
- In some versions, *the Phoenix was shown in flames rather than feathers.*

Another tale….

- The Phoenix lived in Arabia.
- According to the legends only one Phoenix lived at one time and lived for 500 years.
- At the end of its life-cycle, the Phoenix built a nest as it was dying and set the nest on fire and was consumed by the flames.
- After its death, a new Phoenix would then arise from the ashes and the new Phoenix was born. This cycle was repeated over and over.

  - *Phoenix = symbolic representation of the sun.*

And yet, more……

- In Egypt, it was also called the Bennu, said to be a living manifestation of Osiris, springing forth from its heart.
- In Native America, the Thunderbird, a powerful spirit bird is represented as The Phoenix.
- In China, Feng-huang, a bird that symbolizes *the union of Yin-yang. A sign of both peace + disharmony.*

The Greek poet Herodotus wrote in one of his passages from his writings of the Phoenix legend that the Phoenix comes back every 500 years in order to search the body of its predecessor.

- After making a myrrh egg, the Phoenix puts the body of its predecessor inside it, and takes it to the Temple of the Sun located in Egypt.

Mermaids

© 2010, Jupiter Images Corporation

- The sirens (daughters of a Muse) were usually portrayed in Greek art as birds with the head or upper body of a woman.
- They sat on a rock singing sweetly to lure boats astray *over the years, the bird parts changed to fish tails making them mermaids.*

Dragons

- Commonly associated with water
- Classical dragons are frequently guardians of springs *, lakes, bodies of water + treasure!*

Each race had their own type of dragon
- Ancient Egyptian dragons are a *close relation to the crocodile*

- Indian dragons are *elephant dragons*

- Chinese dragons are *stag dragons*

© 2010, Jupiter Images Corporation

Dragonologists and Dragon Slayers of History
Merlin Ambrosius (fifth century AD)

- Considered the founding father of Western dragonology
- Nennius, the ninth-century historian, recounts the story of King Vortigern and Merlin

Edward Topsell

- Seventeenth century AD
- An early English naturalist, included a detailed section on dragons in his scholarly *History of Four-Footed Beasts* of 1607
- *In one note he mentions that dragons are ~~found~~ fond of lettuce but that apples give them stomachaches*

Marco Polo

- Thirteenth century AD

Fire preventer → • Writes about elephant-hunting wyverns, two-legged lindworms, and the methods used to launder asbestos (dragon-proof) clothes in the desert lands of Karakhoja

• *Studied dragons en route to china*

© 2010, Jupiter Images Corporation

George of Cappadocia

• Third century AD
• A dragonslayer who became confused with a Christian saint
• While George of Cappadocia slew an actual dragon , *St. George slew the symbolic dragon of pagenism*

• The dragon George slew was not evil, just hungry. ☺

Beowulf

• Sixth Century AD
• The famous Danish king that was forced to become a dragonslayer when a local dragon was aroused to fury by the theft of a cup from its hoard

Fu Hsi

• 2900s BC
• *First recorded dragonologist.*
• A dragon met him in 2962 BC on the banks of China's Yellow River and gave him the vital secret of writing
• Fu Hsi used writing to teach people how to become civilized

Dragon tidbits....

• Earliest ancestor is the serpent
• Some believe all dragons trace back to one common ancestor Zu: the monster of watery chaos in Sumerian mythology
• In the myths of many races, heroes obtain boundless courage by eating a dragon's heart or drinking its blood, or acquire its penetrating gaze as a result of killing it

• Early Christians thought dragons represented the devil, or antichrist, or more generally, evil passions, paganism, or the oppressive powers of the world
• Chinese dragons frequently appear as the givers of law (western dragons are the takers)

Prehistoric Dragons

• Guesswork and debate
• Very little fossil remains to study

using Darwins theory + working backwards, assume dragons evolved to suit their habitats.

• Fairly small; could fly.
• ∅ sure if they could breathe fire.

- Draconodon

Dragons of Today
European Dragon *(Draco occidentalis magnus)*

- Found in mountains throughout the world, but most common in Europe
- 45 feet long, 13–17 feet tall; compact muscular torso; prominent scales on back, tail and legs; 4 strong legs, 2 bat-like wings, wedge-shaped heads and long necks
- Breathe fire; flame is produced from a combustible venom
- Eat once a month on a sheep, ox, or a human (only if desperate as humans are bitter; prefer virgin maidens)
- *Usually evil, mean and blood thirsty.*

- Also known to have huge hoards of gold and jewels hidden in their lairs
- Color: red, green, black, or gold

Gargouille *(Draco occidentalis minimus)*

- Shares its range with the European dragon
- *Master of camoflage; can remain motionless for hours.*

- Great jumping ability
- 15 feet long, 8–10 feet tall
- Grey or green, hard to spot against buildings/rocks
- Food: rats, bats, and cats; will scavenge from dustbins
- Lives almost exclusively on old buildings—roof tops of ancient castles, chateaus, or cathedrals
- Paris: *Notre Dame cathedral*

Wyvern *(Draco africanus)*

- Lives on the African savanna where the wyvern is the top predator, feeding on elephants and other large herbivores (hippos, rhinos, but will NOT eat giraffes)
- Two early geographers, Herodotus and Pliny both mention the wyvern's taste for elephants
- Usually inclined to being friendly to humans

- 50 feet long, 8–20 feet tall; wing span can be up to 100 feet
- Green to greenish-brown in color
- Most often *depicted in heraldry on shields + banners and is considered a sign of strength to those who bear the symbol.*

Knucker *(Draco troglodytes)*

- Also referred to as a worm
- Found in damp locations, near food sources such as rabbit warrens
- Have only vestigial wings and cannot fly; attacks with venom
- Unless they are starving, safe to approach (adults)

- Hoard household items rather than treasure.

© 2010, Jupiter Images Corporation

- 30 feet long, 3–6 feet tall
- Serpentine
- Color: brown, dull red, or greenish blue skin
- Food: rabbits, farm animals fish; larger ones will eat deer and small children

Lambton Worm

Story about a lazy knight who finds a funny looking worm while fishing
Throws the worm in the well; Worm grows into a knucker and terrorizes the town
Comes back from Crusades to kill the knucker, but causes a nine-generation curse on family

Tibetan Dragon *(Draco montana)*

- Shy beast of great wisdom
- Loves high altitudes
- Known for its hairy armpits; iridescent red or orange in color
- Frozen mountain habitats of Tibet where there are a lot of monasteries; the monks appoint a dragon master to maintain good relations with the local dragon

Chinese Lung *(Draco orientalis magnus)*

- Very benevolent
- One of the longest lived dragons; also called the Imperial lung
- Adept at the human arts; can produce pages of perfectly formed Chinese script and can paint
- 12–15 feet tall, 40 feet long
- Their intellect has allowed them to speak not only Dragonish, but also Russian, Arabic, French, and English as well as several Chinese dialects
- Some have lived up to 1,000 years
- Food: mainly fish and birds; fond of roasted swan or chicken

- During chinese festivals, are often honored w/ dragon boat races & dragon dances.

© Philip Lange, 2010. Used under license from Shutterstock, Inc.

Frost *(Draco occidentalis maritimus)*

- Hard to spot
- Venom is sprayed in a mist through Arctic air and is like frost-bite
- Migrate from North to South poles yearly; prefer winter darkness
- 40 feet long; 12–15 feet tall; spikiest of all dragons
- Color: white tinged with blue or pink; scales are iridescent
- Food: sea creatures such as orcas, giant squid, polar bears, walrus, and leopard seals

Lindworm Dragon *(Draco serpentalis)*

- Two legs, no wings; very long tails and short legs
- Discovered by Marco Polo while crossing Central Asia (inhabits the unpopulated terrain of the Asian interior
- He described them as "Swifter than it looks. Easily able to take down a man on a galloping horse"
- Serpent-like with leathery skin
- 35 feet long; 8–10 feet tall
- Color: pale green or sandy yellow
- Food: bactrian camels, wild horses, snakes for snacks
- Run up to 30 miles per hour

Faerie Dragon

- Very small, any color with large eyes and large butterfly-type wings
- Eat only fruit, vegetables, nuts, and so on
- Rarest of all dragons
- Some myths believe that they come from large butterflies

Hydra *(Draco hydra)*

- Cannibalistic tendencies, preferred food is other dragon's chicks (humans when necessary)
- Have multiple necks and heads (may have evolved to take advantage of rare feeding opportunities)
- Only dragon that reproduces by splitting
- 40 feet long; 10–12 feet tall
- Hercules fought a grand hydra w/ 8 heads
- Jason killed a hydra to get the golden fleece.

Pernese Dragon

- Have four legs and two wings, smooth leathery skin, no scales
- Have telepathic abilities with other dragons and their rider
- Can breathe fire
- Form life-long partnership w/ a human

Drake Dragon

- Legs, no wings
- Two types: Fire and Cold
- Fire breath flames; cold have breathe of snow and hail
- In Europe, there are many cities named after this dragon

Sea Serpent

- Live in water, fresh or salt
- Nessie, the Loch Ness Monster in Scotland
- Seen by sailors, were probably gigantic squids, large masses of sea kelp, or even seafaring dinosaurs

Ouroboros Dragon

- Holds its tail in its mouth
- First discovered in Egypt, later in Greece

Symbol of the universe
"eternity" ; "never ending" ; "infinity."

Manticore

- Composite beast made up of parts of animals with which the audience is likely to be familiar
- Later identified as a tiger with man-face and spiked tail; three rows of teeth

Unicorn

- Possibly a wild ass
- Some say composite of rhinoceros, wild ass, and antelope

Griffins

- Feathered, four-legged animal
- Body of a lion, wings and face of an eagle
- Griffins from Asia and Scythie, who guard the gold and silver, are savage and cruel birds

Chimera

- Fearsome beast
- Head of a lion, body of a goat, and tail of a snake/dragon
- Modern interpretations have given it three heads and dragon wings
- Nowadays, the word is used to describe any fantastic or horrible imaginary creature

Term is also applied by biologists to plants + animals having hybrid characteristics.

Basilisk

- Are shape shifters and so are very hard to spot
- Regarded as the king of serpents

- No antidote for their venomous bite
- No one knows what their "real" shape is like
- Can be killed by the crowing of a rooster, weasels and by seeing its own reflection

Cockatrice *(Gallicus halitosis)*

- Not a dragon as such, but a descendant of the flighted archaeopteryx; also a relative of the semi-mythical phoenix
- Often confused with the basilisk
- Legend says the birth of a cockatrice occurs when a hen's eggs is hatched by a snake or toad

Hippogriff

- Hybrid of a griffin and a horse
- Unlikely, because horse and griffin are mortal enemies

Salamander

- Lizard said to be impervious to fire

  * Cannot be thrown into fire!!!

Sphinx

- Body of a lion and head of a human
- Greek sphinx also has wings
- In Greek mythology, the sphinx poses a riddle to all who seek to pass a rock near Thebes and strangles all who cannot solve it
- What walks on four feet, two feet and three feet, but cannot move well on three and four?

Herodotus

- Traveled throughout the ancient world
- Wrote nine books of History that are named after the Muses
- The Greeks called the nine daughters of Zeus the Muses
- They are the inspirers of various kinds of poetry (tragic, comic, lyric, religious, and epic) and of dance, history, and astronomy.
- Education begins with the Muses because children begin their learning with things musical.
- And...
- Herodotus is the earliest source of the Phoenix and griffin
- Fifth century BC

© 2010, Jupiter Images Corporation

Study Questions

1. This dragon has telepathic abilities and forms lifelong partnerships with a human.
   a. Western
   b. Eastern
   c. Pernese
   d. Drake

2. This ancient animal of India or Persia had a tiger's body, man's face, and spiked tail. It also had three rows of teeth.
   a. Hydra
   b. Chimera
   c. Griffin
   d. Manticore

3. What ancient animal can kill itself just by looking in a mirror at itself?
   a. Chimera
   b. Griffin
   c. Basilisk
   d. Sphinx

4. Which ancient animal is hard to spot due to its camouflage color. He also hides among treetops or sits unnoticed atop the walls of castles and cathedrals.
   a. Wyvern
   b. Western dragon
   c. Gargouille
   d. Hippogriff

5. Which mythical animal was the symbolic representation of the death and rebirth of the sun?
   a. Salamander
   b. Phoenix
   c. Muse
   d. Mermaid

6. Who was the first recorded dragonologist?

    a. Merlin Ambrosius

    b. Edward Topsell

    c. George of Cappadocia

    d. Fu His

7. What dragon is most often depicted on heraldry?

    a. Western

    b. Wyvern

    c. Gargouille

    d. Knocker

end of exam 1.
Ø dates
✓ philosophers.

6 Man as Agriculturalist– Feudal

Objectives

○ To learn about the Dark Ages and Manorial systems that allowed man to survive

○ To understand the role of the church in advancing agriculture

○ To learn about the new innovative inventions that allowed man to succeed in agriculture, such as the plow

○ To realize the beginning and end of knights and their shining armor

○ To understand the importance of wool and sheep production

○ To see how the Black Plague affected agriculture and the way man lived

Feudal

711 AD Moors on Barb horses invaded Iberia
1066 First effective use of stirrups: Battle of Hastings
1098 Cistercian monks taught peasants sheep husbandry
1273 Shepherds organized Mesta in Spain
1327 England became empire of wool under Edward III
1348 Black Plague ravaged Europe
1415 Battle of Agincourt
1454 First how-to book
1492 Columbus brought livestock to New World
1588 Defeat of Spanish Armada

Dark Ages

- As a consequence of the fall of the western Roman Empire, civilization's infrastructure disintegrated
- Trade became impossible because money is no longer backed
- Use of technology changed, beliefs are challenged and take on new dimensions

Manor

- Manorial system came into being
- The manor was a unit of land, including people who lived there
- Over time, the stronger persons exerted control and became lords of the manor
- Manors became as nearly self-sufficient as possible

Horses were necessary to protect manor
- So horses became most important
- Cattle were used for field work

- Swine disposed of household garbage

- Poultry scavenged the barnyards and provided a few eggs

Original manors

- Lords eventually passed control down to offspring—which developed into a hereditary aristocracy
- Peasants or serfs became bound to land with no chance of bettering their position
- Usually one-third of the manor belonged to the lord and was called the demesne and was farmed by peasants for the lord
- Remaining two-thirds of the land was used by peasants

Old manor houses were large structures made of available materials
- Contained a central fireplace and smoke hole in roof
- All families of the manor lived in the house (not much privacy!)
- Sometimes the family of the lord was separated by curtains
- Straw floors, thatched roofs, dog at table for scraps
- They were drafty and cold during the winter

Europe

- During sixth and seventh centuries, plagues ravaged Europe

- Western catholic church was only unity within Europe until ninth century
  Established monasteries
  Churchmen were educated

Confrontation in Central Europe
North:

- Invaded the rivers along the seacoasts of Europe
- Colonized in many areas
- Posed threat from 600 AD to 900 AD

South:

- Tarek the Moor with 12,000 light cavalry on Barb horses defeated Roderick with some 90,000 troops and armored knights who were not well organized
- In 732, Saracens (Battle of Tours) in southern France fought Charles Martel and stemmed invasion of Holy Wars of Islam

East:

- Feudal system was induced by invasion pressures during Charlemagne's reign (late 700s)
- Manors were fortified

"My Lord"

- Feudal system basis was the granting of land by a powerful person to a less powerful one in return for services, usually military
- King→Barons→lesser nobles→serfs

- Freemen held own land or were artisans in growing villages
- This feudal system existed over most of Europe through the Middle Ages and continued for many years

- By this time, the Greeks had invented gears and devices to use water power, but never exploited them because of slave labor
- These were used and running water became available in Europe

Agriculture

- Scratch plow of Near East

- Slavic Moldboard plow

    ○ Because it is so heavy, needed more teams of oxen
    ○ Therefore, cooperation between families occurred

- After 800, three more developments increased output
    ○ Switch from two-field rotation to three-field and use of legumes
    ○ Horse collar came into use from Orient

But…
Use of horses was more expensive

- Feed costs
  Needed to raise oats to feed the horses
  Not as easy to feed as oxen (ruminant vs. nonruminant)

- Textiles
  By 900s utilization of forest land
  Edward the Elder, King of Anglo-Saxons

By 900s, Flanders had become the center of weaving in Europe
Horizontal loom replaced vertical loom (faster)
Spinning wheel increased thread production
From tenth to fourteenth century, industrial revolution occurred in Medieval Europe
Use water-powered mills

Knights

- Henry of Saxony stopped the Huns and made a nine-year truce to fortify cities and build a cavalry force
- After truce, Huns invaded but were defeated
- To keep cavalry in condition, Henry started tournaments (mock wars)

- Two battles that mark beginning and end of the mounted, armored knight
  - Friday, October 13, 1066 Battle of Hastings

  - Battle of Agincourt

The Battle of Hastings

- Harold Godwinson, was given the throne by King Edward the Confessor who was on his deathbed
- Harold becomes the King of England (Saxons)
- Edward had already promised the throne to Duke William of Normandy (Normans)
- William was a bit upset by this and attacked England and Harold

Battle outcome

- Although Harold put up a good fight, he could not withstand William's forces and England falls into Norman control
- During this time, the cavalry was used to its utmost potential and knights were the main defenders of England
- This continued on until the Battle of Agincourt

Mounted warfare = more horses

- The <u>sumpter</u> was a pack horse

- The <u>courser</u> was used by messengers

- <u>Barb and Arabians</u> were introduced and crossed with the courser

- The <u>rouncy</u> was for squires and

- <u>Palfrey</u> was the legacy of the chariot age (pace or racked)

- <u>Andalusian</u> of Iberia

Use of horses produced side effects
- Stirrup became common
- Spears got wings so they would not stick in bodies and pull rider out of saddle
- Saddles got higher cantles and pommels to seat rider better

- Armor was made thicker, but due to added weight, decreased mobility
- Because knights were totally covered, used crests and heraldic trappings for ID

Wars were expensive!

Knights had at least six horses, a page apprentice, smiths, armors, painters, tentmakers, fletchers, cordeners, bowyers, turners, carpenters, masons, wheelwrights, saddles, purveyors, quartermasters, and farriers Plus: surgeons, chaplains, legal and clerical staff, trumpeters, pipers, and cooks!

In between the two battles….. (Hastings + Agicourt)
The horse was used as
- Weapons
- Command post
- mobile throne

- Horsemen
  While European nobles adorned themselves with armor and fought on heavy horses…..
  Steppes of Eurasia housed many thousands of mounted warriors

Great Wall of China
- Completed in 218 BC to protect China from horsemen
- It is said that the ruler Ch'in Ti had the wall built by following the path of a magical white horse
- The wall followed the horse's trail except when a great dust storm engulfed the area
- The builders found, after the storm, that they went too far south and had to change their location

- The extension "oops" is still there

However…
- Even though they had a Great Wall, the Hsin dynasty of China was taken by cavalry in 202 B.C.
- Later, in 1211, Genghis Khan commanded forty Mongol clans and scaled the Great Wall
  - His horsemen plundered Persia, India, and Southern Russia
  - He would attack these areas with a horde of horsemen 10 miles wide, 20 miles long, and each with eighteen horses
- Horses were used for mobility and food
    - mares milk
    - Horse blood
    - Horse steak (carried meat under saddle until it was salted.)
Horse steak

Khan's conquest of China alone decreased the population from 100 million to 59 million
His son Kublai Khan ruled China during 1271–1295, during which time Marco Polo visited

- Interestingly enough
  Horse conquest did not constitute rule over the subjected
  Mongols were absorbed into cultures of China, India, Persia, and Russia

Knighthood

Church induced soldier nobels to become soldiers of the cross.

Established order of knighthood

- The Crusades

    Christians vs. Moors

- The nine Crusades followed
- First four crusades were full-scale wars with religious fervor
    - *Fanaticism*
    - *Massacre*
    - *Terrorism*

- Horses were paramount
    - Richard I
    - Heavier horses of Europe were matched against Arabians and Barbs of Moslems

Flagrant waste of lives and resources, but did awaken Europeans to the fact that the world extended beyond their continent

Trade increased
Spices were imported
Amber, tin, and timber were exported
And….

Cistercian order of monks developed greatest technology for wool production.

Monks taught local people
"Spinster"
- Edward the Elder gave his unmarried daughters this name because all they did was spin wool

Pop goes the weasel.

Trade
Hanseatic League of trading cities was formed
Guilds formed and devised standards for products and craftsmen
Developed apprentice training

Cow milk became more available

Freshness was determined by whether or not it was warm and foamy.

Swine were still primarily garbage collectors

cattle were fattened for slaughter

Ice Age and Plague
Little Ice Age in 1200s for 200 years
During reign of John, signed Magna Carta in 1215
- Crops failed
- Knitting
  - Got more warmth from wool
- Chimneys were used
  - Allowed individual rooms to be heated
- Imported cereal grains to feed livestock
  ← Saved Europe from complete famine.

1348, The Black Death

(caused by ~~ticks~~ fleas →on rats → due to ∅ wolves → due to Spinner.)

- Weakened condition from ice age made it worse
- Estimated loss of 50 percent of population

Sheep
• Sheep were most important, followed by pig (meat + lard) and then the milk cow.

- Edward III, royal wool merchant, laid foundation of the sheep future and wool industry in England
  - He invited Flemish weavers to England (better working conditions, 1337)
  - He taxed wool export and imported wool cloth (to keep wool in England)
  - "wool empire" reached peak during Henry VIII and Elizabeth I reigns
- Henry took property from Church and distributed vast flocks of sheep

- Elizabeth (start of the Elizabethan Age) increased commerce in general
- Changes from medieval to modern England

- Spanish agriculture was also prospering at this time
- Ferdinand and Isabella (1469–1504) organized wool industry of Spain which peaked with Charles V (1516–1555)
- Philip (1555–1598) taxed it to death

The Battle of Agincourt

- Henry V (1413–1422) of England invaded France (100 year war)
- October 25, 1415, The Battle of Agincourt was the beginning of the end of mounted knights
- How did it happen?

The French
- Both armies were in position all night
- French were between two woods and had 25,000 men in a half-mile gap
- It rained all night, so many of the 15,000 knights stayed in the saddle or standing to keep armor mobile
- They were lined up in three ranks

The English
- English, no better off, were outnumbered four to one and were out of food
- But: English dismounted and wedged longbow archers in between the three ranks of the French
- The King told the archers to carve an 8-foot stake pointed at each end. The stake was then driven into the ground at an angle so that when the horses charged, they would be impaled
- Archers fired when French charged and shot down the horses and the knights

The End of the Battle
- Because of the heavy armor that the French wore, many knights suffocated in the mud or were knifed when downed (The English wore an abbreviated armor that made them more nimble)
- Over a short time,
- English lost 500, French 10,000
- Guess who won? English!
- This war plus the plague decreased population

This enhanced the position of the common man, instead of the nobles

Change

1300
    Technology to produce paper in volume
1454
    Gutenberg developed movable type
Fifteenth century
    Spice trade changed
    Columbus discovered New World
    Scholarship and arts changed
Sixteenth century
    Renaissance began in Italy
    Scholars were both scientists and artists
    (Leonardo da Vinci)
    Martin Luther was beginning of the Reformation

Name _online lecture/class_   Date _09/21/11_

Study Questions

1. Which battle marked the beginning of the mounted, armored knight?
   a. Hastings
   b. Agincourt
   c. Huns
   d. Tournaments

2. This mount was the legacy of the chariot age and was used for pleasure riding and hawking
   a. Sumpter
   b. Courser
   c. Rouncy
   d. Palfrey

3. The horsemen that rode with Genghis Khan used horses for mobility and
   a. Companionship
   b. Food
   c. Blockades
   d. They did not use horses, they rode mules

4. In the mid-1300s, after the little Ice Age, what decreased the population by an estimated 50 percent?
   a. Lack of grain
   b. No livestock
   c. The plague
   d. No fuel for heat

5. Who defeated the French during the Battle of Agincourt?
   a. Henry of Saxony
   b. Henry II
   c. Henry V
   d. Henry VIII

6. The Vikings attacked Central Europe from the
   a. West
   b. South
   c. East
   d. North

7. Who stopped the Huns and made a nine-year truce to fortify cities and build a cavalry force?
   a. William of Saxony
   b. William of Normandy
   c. Henry of Normandy
   d. Henry of Saxony

8. Who taught the local people of the feudal times how to produce wool products?
   a. Nobles
   b. Edward
   c. Monks
   d. Knights

7 Man as Agriculturalist– Colonial

Objectives

- ○ To learn how animals came to the New World
- ○ To see how the conquistadores used animals to conquer the natives
- ○ To understand how the Spanish hierarchy in the New World operated
- ○ To learn how the colonies greatly depended on plants and animals to survive
- ○ To see how new crops were used to feed both man and animal

Animal of the day:

Fossa (cryptoprocta ferox)

*pandemic 2.

Colonial
1521 Cortez used horses to conquer Tenochtitian
1540 Coronado accompanied by swine, sheep, and cattle
1550 Plains Indians add horse to culture
1598 Spanish cattle moved across Rio Grande to Texas
1607 Jamestown colonists forced to eat own livestock
1642 English civil war allowed colonists to develop livestock industry
1650 Colonies exported livestock
1776 Declaration of Independence
1783 Shorthorn cattle imported
1793 Invention of cotton gin

Spanish

- Young men of the sixteenth century went exploring the New World
- 1493, Columbus brought new species to West Indies

  Due to ideal conditions, these animals proliferated quickly.

- Actually, they rapid expansion of livestock numbers were almost unbelievable in terms of natural reproductive rates.

Flora of New World

- (corn, potatoes, tomatoes) revolutionized the Old World
- Voyage for horses was difficult
- Horse latitudes of the Caribbean are so named due to the number of horses cast overboard in the calms because of water shortage

  Cattle, swine, sheep, and poultry had 50% survival rate.

The gentlemen of the times were called Caballeros

- Conquistadors with their war horses conquered the American Civilizations
- Horses were necessary because they frightened the enemy the most after God
- The glories of the Inca and Aztec civilizations were no match for the mounted men with morion helmets, steel breastplates, cordovan boots, and pistols

In thirty years, the Spaniards reduced population of New World from 25 million to 1 million. This was in the name of Christianity, to get rid of the cannibalism.

The cannibals would pike the heads of horses and unlucky conquistadors that they killed and ate.

Stallions

- Conquistadors only rode stallions

  Columbus in his old age received special dispensation to ride a mule.

- Had to import mares
- By 1500, the Crown had a ranch with sixty mares
- In less than ten years, many horse and cattle breeding ranches were operating

© 2010, Jupiter Images Corporation

Spanish dons

- The Spanish dons in West Indies prospered more from livestock production than the gold-seeking conquistadors they outfitted
- The ranchers developed an aristocracy that became the envy of all Europe

  Cortez brought livestock to American mainland.

© 2010, Jupiter Images Corporation

- He conquered the Aztecs and started cattle ranching on the central plateau
  Hog raising was easy

  Spaniards ate pork even when they did not have bread.

  (Ate pork to prove they were not Jewish: spanish inquisition.)

Problems

- Initially, very few head of cattle were brought to New Spain (Mexico) to pull carts and plows
- Therefore the ranchers of the Caribbean had a monopoly on providing supplies to conquistadors
- Made it difficult for New Spain to get range cattle
- But, large numbers started coming from Cuba and Santa Domingo and the New Spain ranchers prospered

"New Spain" Mexico, prospered with cattle ranches, sheep and horses 1537.

brand book established to record heraldic symbols placed on hides.

In New Spain, livestock were so plentiful, that a white person out of work could eat and have a horse by simply taking what he wanted

- But land did finally reach a carrying capacity and numbers stabilized
- By 1600 strong European demand for hides
- Merino sheep were promoted late 1500s

1540 Coronado

- Set out in search of treasure somewhere in Southwestern United States
- "Seven cities of Cibola"
- He entered Arizona with 6,500 head of cattle, horses, mules, and swine

1565—Cattle moved to Florida

* many cattle became known as criollo or "cattle of the country."

Vaqueros

- Although the laws of New Spain forbade natives to learn to ride (to keep them subservient)
- Friars trained natives to become vaqueros
- By middle of sixteenth century, horses began to move north in wild band to populate the Great Plains

Horse revolutionalized the Stone Age culture of the Plains Indians

- easier to hunt buffalo (don't have to run them off of cliffs)

Most Indians stole horses
- Nez Perce bred them in great numbers—Appaloosa developed

Cattle
- Many cattle became feral

Over 300 years, natural selection developed the American longhorn

Europe

- Trade continued between New World and Europe
- Sugar (from Caribbean) replaced honey
- Tobacco was imported from Americas by Dutch and English
- Spanish gold revolutionized European economy

1588 defeat of Spanish armada by English gave England rule of high seas

- Merchant class in England began to acquire political power and from 1600 on—formed the East India Company which existed for 350 years

Agriculture in Britain

- Still manorial in nature

- But because:
    - — Cistercian monasteries had been dissolved by Henry VIII
    - — Population reduced due to plague.

- Fixed-rent system
- And parliament's enclosure of common areas
- Landed gentry were prompted to produce English grasses and market it via wool production (clothing was still needed very much by Spanish)

Therefore, sheep raising became more important again

Problems: more peasants became highwaymen, beggars, and if lucky, colonists in New World

New World Survival

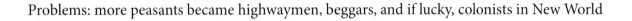

- Survival of the colonists depended on the indigenous Indians of Eastern seaboard
- Forest Indians were "slash and burn" farmers
- Corn was primary crop
- Villages moved every ten to fifteen years
- A forestry area was cleared and burned and corn was planted in hills with squash and beans
- Harvest was on an "as needed" basis, very leisurely
- Diet was supplemented with hunting and fishing
- Indian populations decreased with exposure to European diseases

Britain

- Came to New World 1607
- First colonizing attempts were poor
- Jamestown in 1607 failed
- Tobacco gained a foothold.

3 colonies formed in 1620

- New England
- Middle
- Southern

- Dutch settled in New York in 1614 brought Friesan-type bulls from Holland; trading post in lower Manhattan; *Wall was built to keep animals in: Wall Street*

New England

- By 1636, first meat-packing plant was developed in Springfield, Massachusetts
- 1756—Brighton Market, near Boston, became the first recorded auction market for livestock

Southern Colonies

- Tobacco and cotton (very labor intensive)
- Slaves were used
- Plantations
- Mules was produced in Kentucky and Missouri
- *whiskey production used grain*
- *cattle flourished.*

© 2010, Jupiter Images Corporation

Middle Colonies

- Came later
- Pennsylvania 1681
- William Penn *← centered around him.*
- Good farmland
- Livestock production

Study Questions

1. As the colonies developed more, what was the ideal crop?
   a. Corn
   b. Oats
   c. Wheat
   d. Cotton

2. The single cash crop of the South was
   a. Corn
   b. Cotton
   c. Mules
   d. Whiskey

3. Why was it relatively easy for the Conquistadors to conquer the Incas and Aztecs?
   a. Their Conquistadors' horses frightened them
   b. The Incas and Aztecs just gave up because they were tired
   c. The Incas and Aztecs really like the conquistadors' helmets and wanted to trade for them
   d. The Conquistadors just pointed their pistols and told them to surrender

4. Conquistadors only rode
   a. Mules
   b. Stallions
   c. Mares
   d. Camels

5. Which early colony failed?
   a. New England
   b. Jamestown
   c. Middle
   d. Southern

6. The Spaniards ate a lot of pork because
   a. They liked the taste
   b. It was available
   c. It cooked faster
   d. To prove they were not Jewish

8 Pioneer

Objectives

- ❍ To see how the use of horses is changing
- ❍ To learn how, as the colonies expand, more advances are being made with regard to growing plants and raising animals
- ❍ To learn how animal breeding and selection is becoming more refined
- ❍ To examine how trains and flatboats modernize what people always depended on animals for
- ❍ To see the role of animals in the Civil War
- ❍ To learn how Abe Lincoln started land grant universities

Pioneer
1800 Pioneers crossed Cumberland Gap with livestock
1801 Agricultural societies promoted good animal husbandry
1803 Louisiana Purchase
1820 Missouri Compromise held agriculturally diverse nation together
1827 Erie canal connected agricultural production with markets
1830 "Iron Horse" linked the nation
1837 John Deere plow opened prairie for farming
1849 California Gold Rush
1858 Michigan Ag College pioneered agricultural education
1860 Civil War began

Europe

Gunpowder revolutionized warfare
Knights were replaced by swashbuckling cavaliers with plumed chapeaus, jack boots, pistols, and elegant spurs

European military became infatuated with Oriental Stallion
– State studs were set up all over Europe
– Equestrian skills rose to new heights
– Jockey club and fox hunting

Horses, horses, horses…

- "Sport of Kings" horse racing became more and more popular
- Because so many horses were amassed for wars of the seventeenth and eighteenth century

– Europe became "overhorsed"

– Therefore, Europe became a horse-borne age during Elizabeth I.

- Age of coaches and better post roads and inns

- 1600–1800 (Age of Kings) Europe was war torn
- England and civil war
- New ideas concerning the real importance of people were taking root all over Europe.

Colonies

- Thirteen colonies had advantages over Europe with regard to new government
- Natural resources available seemed endless

* Colonists were enjoying heterosis

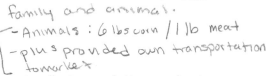

- With energetic people to exploit rich natural resources, success was surely easier

West

- 1783—Tide of pioneers streamed through Cumberland Gap to Ohio Valley and across the South
- 1803—Louisiana Territory was purchased by Jefferson

American pioneer agriculture advanced

- Corn: *near ideal crop. Fed both family and animal.*
  —Animals : 6 lbs corn / 1 lb meat
  —plus provided own transportation to market
- Animals: 6 pounds/1 pound gain
- Plus provide own transportation to market

Subsistence agriculture

- Objective:

- Livestock were integral part of operation
- Yolks of oxen pulled wagons
- Draft horses
- Hogs, poultry, and cattle were trailed with wagon

Transportation

- Flatboats were floated down the Ohio and Mississippi to New Orleans
- Grain, livestock, and timber
- Other water transport was also used
  Great Lakes and Ohio River

Development of infrastructure necessary in Old Northwest to start commercial agriculture

—Markets for food were on Eastern Seaboard where textile manufacture was.

- 1827—Erie Canal was built, connecting Buffalo and Albany
- Cincinnati and Chicago packing plants
- Initially, cattle, swine, and sheep were fattened in Ohio Valley and trailed east to slaughter and the markets
- Drover's inns were located along the routes

1830–1860–U.S. laced together

- Horse-drawn wagons and refined coaches
- *Steam-powered railways revolutionized all of agriculture.*
- Fat stock could be moved to slaughter
- Grain could be shipped to seaports

Importations

- Agriculture in East moved toward livestock production because West was able to supply grain more cheaply
- Dairy production increased in New York *→ Dairy capitol of the world*
- Dutch Holstein-Fresian imported 1852 and 1869
- Berkshire swine from England 1830
- 1860 American swine breed began to appear
  - ○ Poland China (1860)
  - ○ Duroc-Jersey (1865)
  - ○ Corn belt north of Ohio River was center of swine development
- Zebu cattle were introduced into Gulf Coast 1849: coped well with heat
- Vermont: *Merino sheep*
- Boston: *English and Oriental poultry breed*

Areas

- As areas were developed, they spread
- Oregon territory, California, New Mexico, Texas
- Agriculture, especially ranching, in these areas maintained a strong Spanish tradition

Cotton: developed better varieties

- Was very labor intensive
- Slavery increased

Mules were used: *worked harder, better tolerance of humidity*

- Swine for lard and pork
- Some cattle on western edge of the South

Chicago

- 1833 and on: Chicago made transitions
- In 1833, Chicago was a river sandbar with 200 people

- William Butler Odgen, a hustler, helped it to become the hub of commercial agriculture for the entire world
- He brought Cyrus McCormick with his new reaper to Chicago to start International Harvestor

Then the railroads came….

Civil War

- Early 1800s canned food began
- Union army used canned food
- G. Borden made condensed milk
- Preserved by adding sugar

- creameries developed rapidly

End of Civil War, 1865, Union Stockyards in Chicago

Post British Independence

- United States now became a nation bent on growing to fit her seemingly unbounded natural resources
- Old Northwest was breadbasket of country
- East began to industrialize and needed food
- South single cash crop of cotton
- Far West and Southwest: being colonized but had leadership problems

Civil War changed the nation

- Wars devastated the South
- North and West were strengthened producing food and materials for the "new warfare" of civil war

- civil war was very economically influencing

Post-war mounts and horses

- Noble chargers of general officers inspired their men
- Government structures became adorned with leaders on horseback
- Reversed boots in stirrups of an honored man's mount along with lumbering caisson carrying casket symbolized the union of the two

Famous war mounts

- Highfly (Stuart, a dashing cavalier)
- Old Sorrel (Stonewall Jackson)

© 2010, Jupiter Images Corporation

- Traveler (Robert E. Lee)
- Winchester (Philip Sheridan)
- Lexington (William Sherman)

Morrill Act

1862 Abe Lincoln signed the Morrill Act

— Set up land grants for each state to use in the development of agricultural and mechanical colleges for educational purpose

Emigrants streamed West

- Covered wagons
- Primary trails: oregon, California - Overland, + Santa fe

Estimated one-quarter of a million emigrants traveled California trail between 1859 and 1869

1850 Gold Rush
Fort Laramie Register recorded on August 14, 1850:
39,000 men
3,000 women and children
36,000 oxen
7,300 cattle
9,000 wagons

Name _____ Date _____

Study Questions

1. What is the "sport of kings"?
   a. Jousting
   b. Horse racing
   c. Cricket
   d. Soccer

2. What was the near ideal crop that fed both family and animal?
   a. Oats
   b. Wheat
   c. Corn
   d. Potatoes

3. What revolutionized all of agriculture in the mid-1800s?
   a. Packing plants
   b. Auctions
   c. Coaches
   d. Steam-powered railways

4. In the South, what was used to work the fields because they were more tolerant of the humidity?
   a. Mules
   b. Draft horses
   c. Light horses
   d. Oxen

5. What hustler helped Chicago become the hub of commercial agriculture for the entire world?
   a. McCormick
   b. Borden
   c. Ogden
   d. Rockefeller

9 Empire (United States)

Objectives

○ Learn how expansion to the West and trains modernized ranching and moving of cattle

○ To learn about some of the more influential breeders of horses and cattle

○ To examine the true cowboy era

○ To learn how John Deere further modernized farming

○ To learn about the various federal programs for research and teaching

○ To learn about the investors and money men in the various industries of the time

○ To see how life, as people knew it back then, is changing

Empire

1862 Morrill, Homestead, and USDA Acts revolutionized animal agriculture
1865 Chicago Union Stock Yards became hub of livestock industry
1867 Cattle drives began to railheads
1873 Barbed wire used on the Great Plains
1881 *Breeder's Gazette* first published
1884 USDA began livestock research
1887 Hatch Act provided state agricultural experiment stations
1890 Babcock test for milk fat
1895 Trap nesting improved poultry production
1897 National Livestock Association organized

Ranching

- Confederate soldiers returning to Texas after Civil War rounded up unattended cattle (~6 million head)
- In Texas, worth   ~$4 / head

- in East,   ~ $ 20 - 40/head

Joseph McCoy (It's the Real McCoy) from Chicago

- Went to Abilene, Kansas (railhead town) and bought it for $5/acre
- Put the word out to Texas that he would double steer prices
- He originally est. bringing in 200,000 head in 10yrs to Chicago   but actually brought in ↑ 2million in 4 years.

Started the thirty-year saga of trail drives by the American folk legend of "the Cowboy"

- Four famous trails
  — Pawnee
  — Chisholm
  — Pecos River
  — Western

- All trails ended at one of the railheads in Kansas, or in the Dakotas, Wyoming, Montana, and Colorado where they were pastured
- This was the grass left unused after the massive slaughter of the last of the buffalo after the Civil War
- 40 million buffalo GONE!

- Texas longhorn brought cattle fever from ticks infestation.

- Caused deaths of cattle native to Kansas and Missouri

© 2010, Jupiter Images Corporation

During 1870–1880s

- Glamour and profitability of western ranching became famous worldwide
- Money came from the East and overseas, especially Scotland
- Large foreign-owned corporations formed
- In Wyoming alone there were twenty large land and cattle companies and the world renowned Cheyenne Club for the cattle barons

- In SW, ranches of 5,000-10,000 head were common.

© 2010, Jupiter Images Corporation

The XIT ranch in Texas was running 150,000 head on an area 200 miles long and 25 miles wide; used angus bulls, was very progressive

King Ranch in southern tip of Texas contributed large numbers of cattle for both slaughter and to populate range areas of northern states

great internship program.

Huge influence on the horse industry.

Good economics and good weather contributed to ranching boom BUT…….

- Boom ended
  - Winter of 1885–1886 killed up to 85 percent of cattle in some areas
  - Drought in 1887, blizzard in 1888 killed even more
  - Foreign capital was withdrawn or lost
  - Corporation ranches were broken into smaller unit
  - Ranchers began to produce winter feed

1873

- Started using barbed-wire to control pastures
- Many ranchers began to use British breeds (shorthorn, Hereford)
- In first forty years, buffalo were replaced by longhorn cattle, which were then replaced by Hereford
- Cattle production always appeared as a Western enterprise, but in 1880s the Great Plains also had some 12 million head

The "true" cowboy

- The true cowboy was only on the stockman's scene for a short period: 20–30 years

- YET he became an American folk hero of gigantic proportion
  —Being "heir to the long lost cattle Cults of the Mediterranean Basin and the Centaur effect."

Since it was clear that cattlemen were here to stay....

- 1897
- Cattlemen of various states got together in Denver and started National Livestock Association

Range Wars

- Sheep production in high elevations of West and Southwest
- Paralleled cattle ranching
- Wool was primary product
- Range wars between sheep and cattleman were blown out of proportion.
  —sheep graze closer than cattle.
  (Biggest "Beef" between the 2)

Farming

- During same time of 1860–1900
- ~400 million acres of virgin land was plowed
  —Corn, wheat, or other grains
- Corn belt developed rapidly
- John Deere developed steel moldboard plow with rotating coulter was developed
  —could plow matted soil better.

Russians, 1885, brought Turkey Red Wheat

- Grew well in Kansas

More Farming.....

- Chicago was the grain market and livestock center of the world
- Hogs were next and were so profitable, gained the name "mortgage lifters."
- When refrigerated railcars were made, type of swine raised became short, small, and fat (the cob roller); supposedly so the carcasses would not drag on the floor when hung in the (rail)cars.

Chicago

- 1870s there were five big packers around stockyard
- Slaughter costs were paid from by by-products
  - ○ Everything was used
  - ○ Protein animal feed from meat and bone meal
- As railroads extended, new stockyards and plant were built
  - ○ 1871, Kansas City
  - ○ 1873, St. Louis
  - ○ 1884, Omaha
  - ○ 1886, Denver & St. Paul
  - ○ 1887, Sioux City & St. Joseph
  - ○ 1910, Oklahoma City

But Chicago remained the hub...

- Also center of booming purebred livestock business
- 1881, *Breeder's Gazette* was published

Horses from France and Belgium were imported to solve the power problem of Corn Belt farmers

- Chicago had the largest horse and mule sales facility in United States
- 1881, American Hereford Association was established along with
- 1882, Shorthorn ⎤ _Cattle_
- 1883, Angus ⎦
- 1893, Yorkshire ⎤ _Pigs_
- 1895, Hampshire ⎦

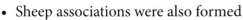

© 2010, Jupiter Images Corporation

- Sheep associations were also formed
- For the first time, livestock insurance was available from places other than Lloyds' of London → _would insure just about anything._

Research

- 1887, the Hatch Act
  - _provided federal funds for development of state agriculture experimental stations._
  - _(Still continues today.)_
- Many of the findings from this research have had a profound effect on the livestock industry

1890, Babcock Test for Butterfat
  — _impetus that began collection of milk records._

- Impetus that began collection of milk records

  More research
- 1895, Trap Nesting

  —Allowed number of eggs produced by individual hens to be recorded.

- 1887, de Laval in Denmark developed the cream separator (great for creameries)

East

- Also time in history when industrial development proceeded in an empire style
- John D. Rockefeller- Standard Oil in Ohio

- Henry Frick and Andrew Carnegie- Steel

- E.H. Harriman- Railroad

- J.P. Morgan- Finance

- Thomas Edison- Investor

1880s–21 million immigrants

- Due to population increase, had to increase food
- American farmers provided it
- First time meat was available to the masses

This is the Wagon that bears the load
Of corn upon the turnpike road ;
Straight from the barn to the mill it goes,
There to be ground, as every one knows,
To make the Quartern Loaf with.

© 2010, Jupiter Images Corporation

- People traveled between cities by Train
  o Within the city, by horse-drawn carriages
  o Team of horses moved produce and goods

    — Teamster unions goes back to heavy ~~horse~~ horse times

- New York City had about 300,000 horses

Study Questions

1. During the 1870-1880s, a lot of money came from the East to form large ranching corporations in the West. Where else did money come from?
   a. Mexico
   b. Washington
   (c.) Scotland
   d. California

2. What ranch made a huge contribution to the horse industry while contributing large numbers of cattle for both slaughter and range areas?
   (a.) King
   b. XIT
   c. Sheldon
   d. Rose

3. The so-called "range wars" were between
   a. Horses and mules
   b. Horses and cattle
   c. Cattle and pigs
   (d.) Cattle and sheep

4. Who developed the steel moldboard plow with rotating coulter?
   a. Ford
   (b.) Deere
   c. GMC
   d. Pontiac

5. What animals were so profitable, they gained the name "mortgage lifters"?
   (a.) Pig
   b. Horse
   c. Cow
   d. Sheep

6. In 1887, what provided federal funds for development of state agricultural experiment stations?
   a. Morrill Act
   b. Smith-Lever Act
   c. Research Act
   d. Hatch Act

7. This allowed the number of eggs produced by individual hens to be recorded.
   a. Trap nesting
   b. Open nesting
   c. Tree nesting
   d. Hen house nesting

10 Man as the Industrialist– Britain

Objectives

○ To learn what events are happening in the animal industry in Britain during the move to the Industrial Age

○ To examine animal breeding changes

○ To learn about Robert Bakewell and his theories for producing a new bloodline of animal

Britain

1700s	Enclosure of manorial commons encouraged livestock breeding
1760	Bakewell set pattern for modern animal breeding
1769	Watt steam engine gave livestock larger market
1783	Bakewell organized Dishley Society, a breed association
1791	Thoroughbred studbook forerunner of herd books
1804	Napoleonic Wars increased demand for livestock products
1822	Coates' herd book recorded Shorthorn ancestry
1840	Scotch Shorthorn developed for beef production
1874	Shorthorn society founded; other breed associations followed

Industrial Revolution in England

- Mid-eighteenth century
- Had it roots in the countryside
- The "empire of wool" during Tudor ties gave the English the experience to capitalize on the massive use of new sources of power to generate goods for an expanding market
- Move from cottage industries to the factory system of manufacture

China dishes

- Josiah Wedgewood produced
- Creamware dishes for commercial use and china for fine dining

Agriculture

- Population increased from 1750 to 1800 in Europe from 140 million to 188 million
- Why?

- Agricultural revolution to produce more food
  - Largely the work of country gentlemen who could afford to experiment and develop
  - Use of wheat, turnips, barley, and clover rotated in fields kept fields productive

- Fertilizers were used
- Farmer's societies and stock shows
- Land closure to control breeding
  - Enclosure gave stock breeders opportunity to select breeding

Eighteenth and nineteenth centuries in England and Scotland

- Important advances in stock breeding
- Breed formation
- Complete enclosure
- Root crops for winter feed
- Improved English grasses

- Large urban markets
Vast needs of Napoleonic wars for livestock production

Robert Bakewell

- Credited with setting the pattern of modern animal breeding
- Deliberate and intense inbreeding of the stock he had gathered
- Probably made wide outcrosses at first (secretly) then went with the inbreeding

- Longhorn cattle
- Leicester sheep
- Shire horses

- Progeny testing young rams
- Created the Dishley Society: objective was to protect the purity of the Dishley Breeds (British Breeds)

© 2010, Jupiter Images Corporation

Breeds

Five steps in typical history of a breed of livestock
- There was a useful type on a given area
- Within this local area, one or more livestock breeders began to inbreed their stock
- Infant breed (which had to survive the inbreeding) had to be popularized over a larger area
- Herd books were published to track breed ancestry
- Breed societies were formed to control herd books

© 2010, Jupiter Images Corporation

Study Questions

1. Who developed china for everyday living?
    a. Bakewell
    b. Cowboys
    c. Wedgewood
    d. Waterford

2. The breeds that were created by Bakewell were referred to as the
    a. Dishley breeds
    b. New breeds
    c. Inbred breeds
    d. European breeds

3. What four crops were used in field rotation to keep the fields productive?
    a. Oats, barley, turnips, clover
    b. Barley, turnips, carrots, wheat
    c. Wheat, turnips, barley, clover
    d. Clover, oats, turnips, barley

11 Man as the Industrialist– Purebred

Objectives

○ To understand all of the aspects that made Chicago the hub of agriculture

○ To learn about the packing industry

○ To explore the Chicago stockyards

○ To see how genetics is playing a role in animal breeding and production

○ To learn about the federal acts that set up experimental stations and Cooperative Extension in each state

○ To examine the various livestock breeds and see how patterns are shifting in their development

1900   First International Livestock Exposition in Chicago
1905   Dairy records (DHIA) gave first data base for selection
1914   Smith-Lever Act initiated extension service
1918   United States in World War I
1920   250,000 miles of railroad joined production to consumption
1929   Stock market crash ushered in Great Depression
1930   Success of hybrid corn caused methods to be studied in livestock research
1938   AI cooperatives used by dairy industries
1939   World War II began
1940   AQHA formed
1945   Atomic Age began
1946   Research and Marketing Act provided regional livestock breeding projects
After
1896: Agriculture began to prosper in United States

© 2010, Jupiter Images Corporation

Chicago

- 1st International Livestock Exposition held at the Union Stockyards at Thanksgiving in 1900

  o *was for fat stock, breeding, and market-ready stock.*

  o Was held after state fairs so it was the culmination of the best
  o Stockmen from around the world gathered to study the prize-winning animals
  o Swine, cattle, sheep, draft horses, poultry

Chicago Union Stockyards

- The largest livestock market in the world since Christmas day, 1865

© 2010, Jupiter Images Corporation

The packing business

- First slaughterhouse, a log structure, was built by Archibald Clybourn in 1827
  o It was situated along the Chicago River and was originally used to kill animals for the supply of the garrison at Fort Dearborn
- There followed a succession of pioneer packers and butchers who built their small plants along the banks of the river

George W. Dole

- Clybourn's successor
- In October 1832, slaughtered and packed 152 head of cattle which were delivered in New York

- The slaughtering took place on an open prairie south of the river, a site now marked by the junction of Madison St. and Michigan Blvd.

Sylvester Marsh

- Another of the pioneers in this business
- Came to Chicago from New England 1833
- Accomplished his first slaughtering operations beneath an old Elm tree on a prairie that is now the west border of the Chicago Loop district at Monroe St.
- The county offered a $1.25 bounty for prairie wolf scalps
- Marsh placed th heads of slaughtered cattle on the Chicago River — Attracted the wolves →easy prey → shot them → got $

Summer packing

- Until now, packing was done in the winter
- In 1860, two houses packed 12,000 cattle during the summer and others put in supplies of ice during the winter so that they could operate the following summer
- This continued to advance Chicago as a cattle market

First regular cattle market in Chicago

- Opened in 1848
- Known as the "Bull's Head Stock Yards"
- On the southeast corner of Odgen Ave. and West Madison St.

1854

- Chicago's population was up to 20,000
- The Michigan Southern Railway opened a yards at the corner of State and 22nd St.
- John B. Sherman opened the Myrick Yards with a capacity of 5,000 cattle and 30,000 hogs
- Other yards began to open on a smaller scale

Centralization

- It became apparent that there was a need for a centralized stock yard to concentrate the scattered yards and to reduce shipping expense and delays
  - Work began on June 1, 1865 and the yard opened that year on Christmas day.
  - 120 acres of pen space
  - $1,000,000 cost was aquired by the railroads.

- Unwise move?
  - The concentration of the livestock business of Chicago at this location was thought by many to be unwise; it was a distance from the heart of the city

    ○ However, this concentration was the most important step ever taken for the benefit of the livestock industry of America (indeed, the world)
- Very important feature
- •A large proportion of the city's working populace found employment.

- It was a prime force in Chicago's rapid growth to a position of fourth rank in population among the cities of the world

Bragging rights

© 2010, Jupiter Images Corporation

- The Chicago Union Stockyards were one mile lone and a half-mile wide
- Boasted a nine-story office building and many other structures
- Nearly 150 miles of trackage
- Railroad equipment
- The country's finest truck unloading chutes
- Cattle pens, sheep and hog houses, horse stables
- Scale houses, grain elevators, sale rings
- Water systems
- And.....
  - ○ New mechanical equipment
  - ○ Specially designed to make the handling of feed and the cleaning of pens the most modern in the country

Success

- Since the stockyards opened in 1865, as of January 1, 1949, a grand total of nearly a billion animals had been sold for a sum of well over $25 billion

International Amphitheatre

- Built in 1934
- 270,000 square feet of exhibit area
- Home of the International Livestock Exposition.

The Stock Yard Inn

- Erected in 1912
- 175 rooms, public and private dining rooms and meetings halls

- Originally built for the accommodation of stockmen having business on the Chicago market.
- Housed the Sirloin room

Saddle and Sirloin Club

- Founded in 1903
- Purpose of establishing a shrine of achievement for the live stock industry

- Portrait gallery
- Closed in 1975 *(officially closed in 1977)*

1890–1920: "Golden Age of Stockbreeding"

- Judging
- Visual appraisal for type
- Type: *Ideal combination of traits that better fits an animal for a specific purpose*

- Linebreeding
  - Breed back to a particular desirable ancestor

upset= only horse to beat Man O' war

© 2010, Jupiter Images Corporation

- Belgian horses
- Man O' War
  - 1924–1947 sired 172 stakes winners

Secretariate had same stride. Ø relation

Technology

- Around 1900 Mendelian genetics used to explain Charles Darwin's Theory of Natural Selection

Explained how heredity passed from one generation to another.

• 1920 Fisher + Wright laid framework

- 1930 J.L. Lush at Iowa State University applied theory of population genetics to improve livestock
  - This revolutionalized stock breed once again

- W.A. Henry (Wisconsin) published "Feeds and Feeding" which became the bible of livestock producers

- 1906, Henry Ford
  - Internal combustion engine
  - 1920s, trucks and tractors started to replace horses

1909, Airplane came about

- World War I horses were used heavily to pull through mud; cavalry was no match for machine guns and tanks.
- Horses were still being used in great numbers during World War I.

© 2010, Jupiter Images Corporation

- High ranked army officers commonly rode horses during World War I.
- Horses and mules were also used to carry heavy equipment to and from the front during the war.

Henry A. Wallace

- Son of a prominent agricultural journalist
- Was curious and pushed researchers at agricultural schools to provide answers for the problems of agriculture
- He later became Secretary of Agriculture who held farmers together during the great depression.
- In 1926, he and others started Pioneer, the first hybrid seed corn company
- 1930s hybrid corn blanketed Corn Belt
- 1930–1940s same principle was applied to cross-breeding both swine and poultry
- Breeding companies were formed that developed lines and crossed them for use in commercial production

Hatch Act

- Provided federal research money for agricultural research.

- But how do we communicate information that is discovered?

Smith-Lever Act of 1914

- Cooperative Extension played a huge role in disseminating new informations to farmers.

  (w/o program, no nation could have expanded its agricultural program like US did.)
- Market News Service (started prior to World War I) helped producers better merchandise stock
- 1921, Packers and Stockyards Act: Protected producer
- 1926, federal grading service graded quality of product

1934–1936–one of the worst droughts

- Plowed prairie land blew away
- Sagebrush took over ranges
- 1920–1930s, over 6 million people (most under 35 years old) left farm never to return

- Transition from rural to urban.

Species

Poultry

- During this time…
  - Poultry production went from farm flocks to near-factory egg and broiler production
  - Cock fighting was still staged

  - Improved electric incubators (1922) created chicken hatcheries which mailed chicks to farmers
    (Based on Ancient Egypt.)
  - Late 1930s saw beginnings of poultry-breeding companies
- Also start of feed companies
- 1944, development of Beltsville Small White Turkey

Use of light to alter laying patterns increased egg production

- Can increase from 150→50 eggs/year

© 2010, Jupiter Images Corporation

Dairy

- 1905, first dairy-cow testing association
- 1927, DHIA—Dairy Herd Improvement Association
- Cooperatives to merchandise milk were formed
- 1938, first AI coop formed

Swine

- 1910, swine were big (as opposed to the cob roller in 1800's)
- By 1930, middle-sized
- 1934, Landrace (Danish) imported to United States
- Development of the confinement unit

© 2010, Jupiter Images Corporation

Beef

- Industry settled into mold
- Calves were shipped to central market, sold to corn belt feeders

- Fat cattle shipped to stockyards, merchandised to packers
- 1930s legislation provided huge tax advantages to invest in the purebred industry

Many things affected the beef industry
- King Ranch (1920s)
  - Developed Santa Gertrudis
    - (3/8 Zebu and 5/8 shorthorn)
  - Charolais breed moved across Rio Grande to Texas in 1936
  - ~~Miles City~~

- Miles City Research Station
  - Reported on cattle trait heritability

- Texas 1941
  - Conducted first bull tests

Horses
- Draft horses moved toward extinction as well as the mule
- "Sport of Kings," thoroughbred racing prospered, as did show horses (esp. Arabians)
- 1940 American Quarter Horse Association (AQHA) was formed
-

Sheep
- Basque Shepards herded western ewes of Merino or Rambouillet breeding at high elevations
- USDA began research efforts to produce sheep with superior wool and more meat
- 1939, synthetic fibers (nylon) were being produced and threatened an already unstable wool market.

Study Questions

1. The first slaughterhouse in Chicago was a log structure. It was built in 1827 by
   a. George Dole
   b. Joe McCoy
   c. Sylvester Marsh
   d. Archibald Clybourn

2. Who placed the heads of slaughtered cattle on the ice of the Chicago River so he could shoot the wolves at night and collect money for the pelts?
   a. George Dole
   b. Joe McCoy
   c. Sylvester Marsh
   d. Archibald Clybourn

3. Who published "Feeds and Feeding" which became the bible of livestock producers?
   a. Mendel
   b. Fisher and Wright
   c. W.A. Henry
   d. Henry A. Wallace

4. What act created the Cooperative Extension Service?
   a. Smith-Lever
   b. Hatch
   c. Morrill
   d. Research

5. What can you use to increase egg production in chickens?
   a. Temperature
   b. Number of chickens/cage
   c. Light
   d. Cage size

6. What invention caused a major decline in the sheep industry?
    a. Artificial insemination
    b. Paylean
    c. Nylon
    d. Confinement units

7. Frozen semen and artificial insemination most greatly influenced which animal industry?
    a. Beef
    b. Dairy
    c. Horse
    d. Sheep

12

Man as a Scientist (Informationalist)

Objectives

○ To learn how the Research and Marketing Act affected animal production

○ To learn how the swine industry was able to select away from stressed hogs

○ To examine the various animal species and see how technology is changing their production and management

1952 Freezing bull semen from superior sires
1953 Discovery of DNA structure
1954 Performance Registry International began
1955 Layer and broiler confinement industries separated
1957 Sputnik triggered increased interest in science and livestock research
1962 Milk production began dramatic increase through sire evaluation
1965 Computer technology revolutionized livestock data analysis
1967 Many beef breeds imported through Canada
1968 Beef Improvement Federation formed
1975 National Swine Improvement Federation formed
1980 Beef sire evaluation demonstrated genetic trend for growth

© 2010, Jupiter Images Corporation

Atomic bombs dropped on Japan ended World War II

World entered a new age

1946 Research and Marketing Act

- Worked on problems applicable to regions of the United States
  ○ Two regional projects on beef cattle breeding programs
  ○ Two regional projects on dairy cattle breeding
  ○ One project on poultry breeding
  ○ One project on sheep breeding
- Already had a swine breeding program intact that the other new programs were based on
- Program was successful

Animal Numbers

Swine

- By late 1950s, 80 percent of market hogs were crossbred hogs that still carried a lot of fat

  – This fat was essential to the war
  – After war, efforts were made to decrease fat

- 1956, Iowa boar-testing station was built

  – Used back-fat probe to evaluate fatness
  – Promoted use of boars w/ less fat

- By 1960s, some muscular pigs were stress prone
  — Would die on way to market

- L. L. Christian discussed this with medical researchers and found that on occasion, human given halothane gas were stressed and died
  — Based on this, he developed a halothane screening test for ~~the~~ young breeding stock.
  — This test was able to eliminate carriers from breeding programs.

- Since then, swine are selected for increased size with optimum fat, without being overdeveloped

New problems in the swine industry

- Paylean and oxygen

- Total confinement units and waste control

© 2010, Jupiter Images Corporation

Dairy

- American dairy industry produces 2.4 times the milk that it did during World War II from 46 percent of the cow numbers

- AI and milk records helped to improve production.

Frozen Semen

- 1952, discovered that bull semen could be frozen and stored in liquid nitrogen
- This really influenced the breeding of dairy animals

- As computers arrived, dairy industry was the first of animal industries to use it for data collection and evaluation

Poultry

- By 1960, complete confinement with light control egg processing
  — Candling
  — Grades
  — boxes

Sheep

- Has problems
- Between 1945–1976, sheep numbers fell by 38 million head

- Volatile wool market, plus competition from Australia and New Zealand can be blamed.

- Synthetics replaced wool.

© 2010, Jupiter Images Corporation

- Volatile wool market, plus competition from Australia and New Zealand can be blamed

- Lamb consumption has decreased
- Sheep industry is booming in New Zealand and has made profound contributions to the development of world nations

Beef

- 1950–1975, Per capita consumption increased
- Market animals fed in feedlots
- End of purebred epoch was traumatic
- Extreme selection for compact bovine increased the incidence of a dwarf genes

- Mid 1950's sought for dwarf free animals

- Central bull tests
  – Found and propagated based on performance

- 1945–1950, extension beef cattle improvement programs were started
- 1955, Performance Registry International (Texas) was formed
- 1960s, nearly 80 percent of beef cattle were being fed as a result of southwestern commercial feedlots

© 2010, Jupiter Images Corporation

Horses

- Horse numbers have increased dramatically over last few decades

  – 1975 International Livestock Exposition closed its doors
  – Now: North American International and the Denver National Western Stock show carry on the tradition.

– Became focal point of industry for performance cattlemen

– First breed association to require weaning performance for registry was Red Angus Association.

Study Questions

1. After World War II, which act provided for the creation of regional research projects that encouraged larger animal research efforts?

   a. Hatch Act

   b. Smith-Lever Act

   c. Morrill Act

   (d.) Research and Marketing Act

2. How can we tell that the pig we are breeding is not too fat?

   a. Slaughter his progeny

   (b.) Back-fat probe

   c. Poke-in-ribs probe

   d. By weight of the pig

3. Some muscular pigs would die on the way to market. What did Christian do to help prevent this problem?

   a. Stopped breeding the sows that these piglets were out of

   b. Gave them an exercise-stress test

   (c.) Gave them halothane gas to test for the stress gene

   d. Just did not sell any pig that looked like he was to muscular

4. What was used to alter laying patterns to increase egg production in chickens?

   (a.) Light

   b. Cage size

   c. Music

   d. Comfy pillows

5. What is one of the major problems facing the swine industry today?

   (a.) Waste management

   b. Housing shortage

   c. Stress syndrome pigs

   d. Profitability

6. Which of the following really influenced the breeding of dairy animals?

   a. Candling

   (b.) Frozen bull semen

   c. Embryo transfer

   d. People stopped drinking so much milk

13

Exotic Animals and the History of Zoos

Objectives

○ To learn about historical collections of exotic animals

○ To understand the difference between a menagerie and zoological garden

○ To see how the people of certain areas treated exotic animals

○ To learn about the first modern zoo

○ To learn how Versailles and Vincennes in France made an impact on exotic animal collections

○ To see the progression to the more modern day zoo and how it developed

○ To learn the five main reasons why we have zoos today

Gardens of History

Ancient World

- Large Babylonian, Chinese, and Greek collections
- Exotic animals were kept by all sorts of Roman emperors, governors, and statesmen
- Alexander the Great, emperors Trojan (collection of some 11,000 animals) and Nero

Eighth Century

- Charlemagne owned a large menagerie
  — King of the Franks

- Undisputed ruler of Western Europe
- Realm encompassed what are now France, Switzerland, Belgium, and The Netherlands, half of present-day Italy and Germany, and parts of Austria and Spain

CHARLEMAGNE.

© 2010, Jupiter Images Corporation

Twelfth and Thirteenth Century

Large collections in France, Italy, the German-speaking countries, and England
King Henry I (son of William the Conqueror) started English royal tradition of keeping exotic animals at Woodstock

— Collection was moved to Tower of London by Henry III

mid nineteenth century: poor remnants of collection were transferred to new Zoological Gardens of London in Regent's Park

Sixteenth Century

Thousands of animals belonging to Akbar, the third mogul emperor of India and Montezuma's huge collection on Tenochtitlan

Eighteenth Century

Clara, the rhinoceros traveled 1741–1758 throughout Europe
She was seen, drawn, and studied

All the 'rage'
women even had rhinoceros hairstyles

© 2010, Jupiter Images Corporation

Eighteenth-century Paris

- Exotic animals had a major presence in Paris
  - On the street; in private homes; in jokes, poems, stories, posters, paintings, and in work of natural history. Often took on metaphorical meanings when transformed to literature or art.

- <u>Where did they stay?</u>
  - King's menagerie
  - Fairs and fights
  - Bird-sellers' shops
  - Private homes

How did the animals get to Paris?

- By ship, but this was not always easy or successful

- Were eaten if food was scarce, or were killed/eaten if food for the animals ran out

- Initially animals were collected dead by the naturalists who preserved them for museum specimens
- Then as time went on, many foreign dignitaries presented visitors with live animals with the intention that these animals be taken back and presented to their king (tigers, monkeys, birds)
- But, as menageries became popular, kings could not depend on just gifts to fill the cages, so they commissioned agents to supply animals

Louis XIV

Gave standing order for exotic species

Built the new menagerie at Versailles between 1687 and 1694
A purveyor brought at least 900 animals to Versailles, including more than 100 ostriches and 500 purple swamphens

Louis XV

Showed less interest in the menagerie, but continued to accept gifts

Included tigers, a rhinoceros, and an Asian elephant

Louis XVI

Revived the animal park (1782) after the American war disrupted trade of animals

King sent out requests for species he lacked.

A lot of captains would not take these animals onboard because

They ate too much
Took up too much room, etc.
In addition to the animals consigned by the king, many others were brought

- Many of these were spoken for and to get one, you had to have had an inside connection.

By the end of the eighteenth century...

It was suggested that animals be imported more systematically

This was followed by the recommendations for proper shipping (birds)

Send in pairs
use appropriately sized cage(s)

Send you tame birds, not grown, wild ones
Teach them to eat in the cage before sending them
Cages should be built to minimize injury

© 2010, Jupiter Images Corporation

The Royal Menagerie

Until now, the royal animals were moved around from palace to palace on the whim of the king; however, Louis XIV built two menageries

1.) Vincennes

- Lions, tigers, and leopards were kept in cages around amphitheater where king could entertain courtiers and visiting dignitaries with bloody battles
- Ex: *In 1682, the Ambassador of Persia enjoyed the fight to the death between a tiger and an elephant.*

(Both ended up dying due to injuries)

2.) Versailles

- Very different
- Displayed peaceful animals
- Centered on a small chateau with an octagonal observation room

- *Perfect example that animals were caged for human amusement and as symbols of status and power.*

- Around 1,700 occupants
- Storks and sheep; cranes; large birds from Asia and Africa; wading birds, various other birds
- Ostriches, eagles, porcupines, and other small animals; cassowaries, elephant, and camels
- Domesticated animals raised for king's table

The Menagerie at Versailles

Where was it?

- Located about two hours outside of Paris by carriage or horseback
- Public coaches took about four hours, were packed with people
  - *Took longer because coachmen would stop at every inn along the way for a drink.*

© 2010, Jupiter Images Corporation

The Academians

- A group of researchers was started and financed by the king
  - studied animals
  - Especially interested after death

- Would even have anatomical exhibits after dissection
- The king himself showed up for an elephant dissection

Vincennes to Versailles

- Eventually, the lions, tigers, and leopards were transferred from Vincennes to Versailles where they were then housed
- After Louis XIV death, Louis XV had little interest in animals
- Although the menageries were maintained, the academians were no longer paid and funded to do dissections and studies.
- Any new animals gifted to the king continued to go to the menagerie

      Louis XVI

  - Groomed his public image and used the menagerie once again

- Visitors began to see site as a natural history observatory, although it also received more criticism from public
- The animals changed all the time: rhinoceros, zebra, musk deer, aquatic birds, etc.

Late 1700s

- Menagerie fell into disrepair and the animal population decreased
- War in the Americas meant fewer animals being available and/or shipped
- Even though the treasury was low, the king got loans to rebuild and restock in 1780s

- This still shows the importance they put in the menagerie.

- Acquired some interesting animals including panther, hyenas, tigers, badgers, ostrich, mandrill, monkeys, zebras, and lions

Changing Times

- Many people began to look down upon menagerie
- Naturalists said the animal behavior could not be studied because settings were not natural
- Animal's lives were shortened due to lack of proper nutrition and exercise
- Because of growing commercial traffic and increasing flow of exotic animals, urban menageries began to rival the collection at Versailles

Jardin des Plantes

- About 1794, Versailles menagerie was emptied of last few remaining animals which went to Jardin des plantes

- Meanwhile, back in Paris, 1760ish, there were many animals on display in Paris itself
- Lions, elephants, baboons, cockatoos, and many other species were on display in booths at city fairgrounds or along boulevards
- Bears and monkeys could be seen dancing and doing tricks.

- Some of the animal collections rivaled those of the king

Combat d'animaux

- Bloody show featuring bulls, deer, bears, boars, and wolves
- Lions, tigers, leopards, polar bears, and mandrill would take turns facing trained attack dogs
- These fights disappeared around 1833

Oiseleurs (bird sellers)

Definitions

"Menagerie" describes collections of captive animals kept "simply" for purposes of display or for the aggrandizement of the owner; contained "caged animals"

"Zoological gardens" are places that provide scientific endeavor and public education

Fictional animals thrived in seventeenth- and eighteenth-century literature

- La Fontaine's fables
- eleven books of fables, 1668–1679
- fables reveal a perceptive, worldly wisdom and received the greatest acclaim
- most of the fables feature animal characters but convey insights about human behavior

- First public zoo in 1793 in Paris :

  Jardin des Plantes

- This was followed by
  - 1828, Zoological Gardens of London
  - 1843, Gardens of Amsterdam

○ 1844, Berlin
○ 1862, Central Park, New York

Zoological Gardens

- Education
- Science
- The possibility that the collections could become centers of emerging environmental and animal protection movements
- Basic human need for nature in the midst of urban concentration

Zoos

- Initial zoological collections were for power and status
- Nineteenth and twentieth century represented a genuine interest in animals
- Zoos have gone from being "freak shows" where animals were on display to places where animals are treasured and supported

Hagenbeck Revolution

- Beginning of twentieth century
- Modern zoo design
- Take animals out of cages and put on display in natural setting.

Carl Hagenbeck

- Mid-nineteenth century began buying and selling exotic animals in Germany

- Not only traded animals, also people, from all over the world.

- late 1880s, he began to exhibit a series of unique animal acts
- The animals had been trained in new and humane ways
- In 1907, animal business, people exhibitions, and performing animal acts had permanent home in northern Germany
- A zoo without iron bars

Hagenbeck Period

- Emphasis was on the animal exhibit, with Hagenbeck himself not having any pretensions about science or education
- Showed how animals co-existed with one another in an ecosystem

Progression of Zoo Types

- Royal menageries
- Linnaean taxonomy
- Hagenbeck panoramas
- Zoogeographic arrangements
- Modernism
  - Abstraction
  - Realism
  - Landscape Immersion

Linnaean taxonomy

- About 1735 the Linnaean classification had a profound impact on the organization and interpretation of zoo collections
- Also made curators realize they had "gaps" in their animal collections which led to a rush to complete the collection

Zoogeographical Arrangements

- Tried to arrange collections geographically (based on where animal lived)
- Benefit was that it gave visitors a clearer picture of the animal's ecosystem and the inter-relationships between one animal and another and its habitat

Modernism

- with the increase of professionals (engineers, architects, designers, etc.) enclosure design has suffered

- While outdoor exhibits still had the Hagenbeck influence, rockwork as abstract expressions of natural forms got changed to plain walls of concrete and masonry
- Indoor exhibits, due to issues of health and sanitation, became glass-fronted, laboratory like enclosures lined with tiles and equipped with stainless steel furnishings

Post Modern

- High-tech exhibits
- Example: live penguin exhibit is so long, a conveyor belt carries visitors while inside, snow is manufactured to keep the temperature cold for the birds

Immersion Exhibits

- Last two decades
- Emergence of exhibit design reconciles both need of animal and visitors

  - Zoo director sees his job as a conservationalist

- Visitors think the zoo owes them spectacular entertainment
- An immersion exhibit, an enclosure design in which the visitor feels "immersed" within the enclosure
- No sense of barrier
- Enclosure is landscaped with the use of both real and artificial material giving an extremely real impression of the animals' habitat

Why do we have zoos?

Five main reasons
- Conservation
- Reproduction
- Education
- Research
- Recreation

Conservation

- Safe haven for endangered + threatened species

- Conservation, which includes reproduction, also consists of the rescue and preservation of existing animals
- Some zoos participate in conservation projects outside their walls
- Example: sponsor efforts to preserve natural habitats

Reproduction

- Between 2,000 and 6,000 animals species will become extinct in the near future without human intervention
- Captive breeding has saved several animals, including European Bison, Hawaiian Goose, and the Arabian Oryx (antelope)

- Zoos trade and lend animals to avoid inbreeding

- Many participate in the International Species Information System (ISIS) which documents genetic background

Education

- Most modern zoos believe primary mission is to educate the public
- Teaches not only about animals, and our relationship with them, but also about our place in the natural world
- Many now offer distance-learning programs online

Research and Recreation

- Daily observations of animals allow behavior studies and physical observations
- If you know what animals will tolerate and what is normal, you can help them if they get sick or hurt
- Entertain both adults and children

- Over 134 million people visit zoos yearly

Modern Zoos

- Not a "living museum" but a place where animals should feel at home.

- Latter part of twentieth century, zoos began to provide new visitor experiences by replacing iron bars and concrete walls of cages with protective moats, bigger animal areas, and recreated tropical rainforests
- San Diego Zoo, 1916, helped pioneer this shift

First Zoos in United States

- 1868, Chicago's Lincoln Park Zoo
- Closely followed by Philadelphia Zoo and New York Central Park Zoo

- What we know and where we are going.....

- 1907, Carl Hagenbeck created Tierpark in Hamburg, Germany, used moats, but this took a few years to catch on elsewhere
- San Diego in 1922 opened the first lion exhibit free from wires in United States
- Today, Bronx Zoo "Wild African Plains" exhibit shows how this technique offers a seamless view of animals co-existing but deep gullies separate them
- And....
- Since 1960s, zoo horticulturists have built naturalistic habitats
- Designers must face issue of insect control, drainage, plant toxicity, durability as well as depicting the animal's natural habitat accurately and providing an interesting environment
- Animal health care another important mission of zoos

Study Questions

1. Which of the kings of France could care less about the exotic animals and let the menageries go into disrepair?
   a. Louis XIV
   b. Louis XV
   c. Louis XVI
   d. Henry I

2. Which menagerie was closed to the public and was for blood sport?
   a. Versailles
   b. Vincennes
   c. Jardin des Plantes
   d. Tower of London

3. Which menagerie was for peaceful animals that the public could visit?
   a. Versailles
   b. Vincennes
   c. Jardin des Plantes
   d. Tower of London

4. Initially, zoological collections were for
   a. Education
   b. Research
   c. Power and status
   d. Money

5. An oiseleur is a
   a. Bird seller
   b. Monkey peddler
   c. Bear dancer
   d. Lion tamer

6. Which of the following is not one of the modernist progressions of zoo types?
   a. Realism
   b. Abstraction
   c. Linnaean
   d. Landscape immersion

7. What had a profound impact on the organization of zoo collections, and made the curators realize they had "gaps" in their animal collections?

    a. Zoogeographical arrangements

    b. Linnaean taxonomy

    c. Modernism

    d. Hagenbeck panoramas

8. Where was the first zoo in the United States located?

    a. Chicago

    b. New York

    c. Philadelphia

    d. San Diego

14 Animism and Totemism

Objectives

○ To learn how animals were perceived and symbolized throughout ancient times

○ To see the unique ways man used animals to represent their history

○ To learn about totemism and how it evolved

○ To learn about the various totem poles and their roles

*online survey   -suggest Kinkajou.

Definitions

- Animism: "Any of various primitive beliefs whereby natural phenomena and things animate and inanimate are held to possess an innate soul."

- Totem: "An animal, plant, or natural object serving among certain primitive peoples as the emblem of a clan or family by virtue of an asserted ancestral relationship."

- Totemism: "The belief in kinship through common totemic affiliation or the identification of an individual or group with a totem."

Animals appear in three realms or orders

- Biological (literal)
- Psychological (imaginable)
- Conceptual (symbolic)

© 2010, Jupiter Images Corporation

Animalizing

ex:
-Mascots
-Cartoons

- When animals take the form as primarily nonbiological beings
- They become a vehicle for the human imagination to soar
- This is a form of imagination called "animalizing"

Shamanism

- The practice by man of animalization
- The shaman is the human that is most readily animalized.

Example

- The animal serves as the totem for the animal rights movement

Animism and Totemism

- Have their basis in man's journey into the creation of psychological and symbolic animals
- Pigs were considered sacred by several early civilizations
  - the Egyptian culture through the goddess Nut,
  - the Greek Mother and Daughter pair Demeter and Persephone
  - In Celtic myths, humans and pigs were interchangeable (shape-changing), and the pig was often reffered to as immortal.

- The pig was sacred to many early societies
  - South East Asia, Pacific Ocean islands, West Africa, and Europe, and each culture had mythologies about pigs
    - For example, there were cultural ties between the sacrifice and consumption of pig flesh with human female purification rites.
    - The taboo of eating pig flesh by God in Leviticus, led to some cultures believing that the eating of pork brought wisdom, as they believed pigs must be gods.

  - In The Odyssey, Homer tells of the magical intervention of the sorceress Circe who turns Odysseus' men into swine. They are swine in body only, as they obtained the mentality of men.

Examples of Animism in Man's History

- Guinea Indians of Guiana, in South America
- Instead, they regarded much of the natural world as being gods
- The Guinea's believed that all animals were descended from the snake and the tiger.

A folktale from the Carib People

- A woman from the Warrau tribe went into the jungle, and there met a large water-camudi snake, who could change from man to snake. The snake would crawl up a tall tree full of fruit, change into a man, and shake the tree for the woman to collect the fruit. Then the man would become a snake again and slither back down the tree. The woman and the snake-man mated, and by and by the

woman had a snake-child, which she hid in the jungle. Her family became suspicious, and one day her brothers followed her. They saw her making love to the snake and playing with her snake-son. When she left, her brothers caught her lover and son and slaughtered them, carving them up into many pieces and throwing the pieces far into the jungle. Sometime later, the brothers were on a journey through the jungle and heard the noise of a village. There, where they had thrown the pieces of snake, was a new village full of men, women, and children. These humans had sprouted from the body of the dead snakes, and they became the ancestors of the Carib tribe.
- Animism was a strong belief among the tribes, with both animate and inanimate objects being given human characteristics and abilities

Shamans, Spirit Animals, and Familiars

- Shamans each have an animal "familiar" who is their guide in the spirit world

- *There are many stories of the introductions of man and spirits beast throughout the literature and lore of ancient tribes, particularly from the Artic Circle area.*

Example

- An Inuit shaman told his story of initiation as a shaman:
  - While out hunting, a huge walrus tipped his boat over. The walrus pulled him deep under water and severely gored him, puncturing his lung and breaking his collarbone. The hunter managed to make it home, where the local shaman healed him. The hunter then became a shaman himself, with the walrus as his familiar.

- Through the power and savagery of the animal connection, the shaman gains his power, including the power to heal.
- They learn to mobilize the power of terrible fear and turn it into the ability to treat the sick of their tribe, and to take the evil spirits away from the sick person.
- In parts of the world where shamanism has existed since earliest recollection, members of the tribes believe that the invisible world of spirits can also be an unseen force indwelling natural phenomena, similar to the beliefs of the Guinea Indians we discussed earlier.
  - The San hunters of southern Africa address the rain as a "beast of prey" and compare it to the cobra and puff adder. The rain is said to pelt people with the meat of these snakes.
  - *Similarly, the Aborigines of Australia fear dangerous animals that they percieve in the landscape. These are not natural animals, but dream monsters that attack the soul.*

Totemism: Animals as Signs

- The word totem (aoutem) was first seen in modern written language in France in the early 1600s.
- It came from the trips of many explorers to the upper North American continent, and was used to refer to native tribes' familiar spirits.

- *Early accounts of totemism counted as a religion, with animal spirits being scared to the peoples involved.*

The following conditions had to be met to fall under the classification of totemism:

- The genealogy of the group of people must trace, in the tribes mind, from a common animal ancestor.
- An animal spirit serves as a guide or educator to the tribe or person.

- The human-animal relationship is representative of the tribes being in tune with the world at large.
- There is evidence of the belief that humans and animals had at one time a closer than normal relationship—i.e., ability to co-mingle in love and marriage.

- Totemism deals primarily with the idea of animals as conceptual signs, seen in the mind.
- The concept is very like shamanism, with animal familiars
- Many primitive tribes practiced totemism, which is a form of animal worship.
- In general, the differation made between familiar and totem, is that the former is an individual association, and the latter usually refers to a group association.

Egypt

- One of the earliest cultures to practice totemism was Ancient Egypt, where animals played a key part in their religion.
- Many animals were linked with gods and goddesses
    - Buto of Lower Egypt
    - Bastet, cat goddess
    - Anubis, the crouching jackal
    - Hathor, the cow

- The religious imagery of Egypt included the ability of the same deities to be represented as animals, men, or men with animal heads.
- Egyptians used many totemic images, with birds, cats, and ibex among the most common animals to be made into images. → From carved rock toys to the sphinx (½ man ½ cat)
- Clans had their own totemic images and placed the image of their clan on their ships standards and on their household pots.
- Totem animal images were also included in the tombs of ancient Egyptians. All providences had their own animal gods, and their animal totems were depicted in their provincial centers.
- These totemic associations lasted well into the age of Christianity.

Totem Poles

- The function of totem poles was not to serve as objects of worship or to honor the animals that were often carved on them. Instead, the pole serves as an emblem of honor for a person or family.

© 2010, Jupiter Images Corporation

- Generally, they are historical monuments or documents of great meaning and value to the culture that carved them.
- They displayed a people's origins and lineages, their supernatural experiencess, their exploits and achievements, and their success.
- These recorded histories gave the people a cultural identity and proclaimed their wealth and status in the village and tribal group.
- The most prolific area for creation of totem poles is the N.W coast of N. America

- An important part of their tradition was rooted in the people's understanding of their close association with all living things and their dependence on members of the plant and animal kingdom for their survival in an often harshly cold land.
- Their dependence on certain plants and animals fostered their belief in the supernatural, and they had a deep belief that all life forms taken for their use as food, shelter, or clothing each had the breath of spirit, just as humans did.

- Tales of contact with animal and plant spirits were passed down from generation to generation.
- To ensure that the peoples did not forget their this story and legends, carvers would take great poles and carve humans, real/imaginary animals into them.

Potlatch

- The raising of a totem pole was a special event that called for a ceremonial party called a potlatch
- The poles would be placed next to their houses and represented the families who dwelt in them and their individual histories
- In the 1800s, totem poles came to represent wealth and status, rather than symbolism of the tribe
  o Fur Trade had become very profitable for the people of the N.W and chiefs, noblemen among the tribes would commission the finest carvers to creates bigger and more elaborate poles to adorn their houses.

- In the 1860s the fur trade began to wane, and so did the production of poles

Christianity

- Then Christianity arrived, changing many of the tribes' beliefs, and poles were felled to rid the villages of what white man saw as profane symbolism of ancient godless beliefs.

- In 1884, the Canadian government outlawed the potlach

- Carvers died, and no one trained to take thier place, so no new poles were created.

- Poles were also sold or stolen by collectors who would sell artifacts to the museums of America and Europe.
- Between the 1870s and 1920s, hundreds of poles were purchased and removed from vacant villages without permission of payment and went to New York, Chicago, London, New Zealand, and museums in eastern Canada.
- Pole collecting continued into the 1970s, nearly completely decimating poles from their natural homes.
- Finally, in 1951, the potlatch ban was lifted and carving of totem poles was re-initiated as part of the old tribal traditions which came back to life.

- Today, totem poles are carved + raised accompanied by the ancient potlach
    - lost symbolism

What were they made of?

- Totem poles were and are carved primarily from the trunks of western red cedar trees and can reach over 100 feet in height.
- A number of different types of totem poles were carved for various purposes in the villages of the 1800s

Types of totem poles

- Welcome pole
- House posts
- House frontal poles
- House portal pole
- Memorial poles
- Mortuary poles
- Shame poles
- Commercial pole

© 2010, Jupiter Images Corporation

Welcome Pole

- Set up near the village beach.

- Welcome poles portrayed a larger-than-life human figure w/ arms outstretched to welcome visitors arriving for a feast or potlatch.

House Posts

- Were placed inside the houses of high-ranking chiefs
    - These were carved with emblems of family history

House Frontal Poles

- Were placed outside of a family's house with the doorway to one side of the pole
    - Pole carried the histories and crests of the family, proclaiming their ID, worth, and social standing

House Portal Pole

- Similar to the frontal pole, but has an oval entrance cut through the base
- This special entrance was used only on ceremonial occasions for Processional entry into the house.

Memorial Poles

Took 1 yr to carve

- Stand in front of the house, but were not attached to it
- This pole would have a single crest at the base or top, and would be elaborately carved along its length
- These poles commemorated the life of a chief and were raised about a year after his death
- Figures representing special achievements and events were carved on the pole.
- The new chief would give a potlatch for the raising of the Pole.

Mortuary Poles

- Were carved for persons other than chiefs who were of high rank in the tribe
- After the person's death, the dead person was placed in a fancy, carved box and placed in a mortuary house for one year.
- After a year, the decayed remains were removed and placed inside of the Mortuary Pole, which was carved with the crests of the person who died.

Shame Poles

- Have no remaining representatives except in museums
- These poles were carved for a chief who wished to ridicule and shame another person, usually a rival
- A misdeed or long-standing rivalry was publicly proclaimed by the rising of the Shame Pole
- The pole would show the person to disadvantage
- Fortunately, the poles were taken down when the controversy was over.

Commercial Pole

- These are commissioned poles, but they still resemble the true poles.
- Special ceremonies are held in the place- museum, bank, hotel, etc. where they are raised.

The Figures in the Totem Pole

- Human and human-like beings may be carved either standing up or in a crouched position.
- 4 legged animals such as bear or beaver can be carved in similar positions.

- Birds are usually carved as being on a perch with their wings outstretched, legs have clawed feet, and their beaks may extend horizontally from the pole or be carved as being against the birds chest.

- Poles are read from the top down, and contrary to the saying "top man on the totem pole," the top figure is not the most important, in fact just the opposite.

  – Most important = bottom

- The crest is found at the top of the pole and this image proclaims the person's linage and heritage.

  —Many creatures are found as crests. Many are mythical, such as the Thunderbird, and other similar mythical birds.

- In addition to totem poles serving to tell the real history of a family, they were also used to depict legends that were passed down from generation to generation.

Study Questions

1. Any of various primitive beliefs whereby natural phenomena and things animate and inanimate are held to possess an innate soul is the definition of what?
   a. Totem
   b. Totemism
   c. Animism
   d. Animalizing

2. An animal, plant, or natural object serving among certain primitive peoples as the emblem of a clan or family by virtue of an asserted ancestral relationship is the definition of?
   a. Totem
   b. Totemism
   c. Animism
   d. Animalizing

3. The belief in kinship through common totemic affiliation or the identification of an individual or group with a totem is called?
   a. Totem
   b. Totemism
   c. Animism
   d. Animalizing

4. When animals take the form as primarily nonbiological beings and become a vehicle for the human imagination to soar, it is called
   a. Totem
   b. Totemism
   c. Animism
   d. Animalizing

5. The practice by man of animalization is called
   a. Beastiality
   b. Simonism
   c. Shamanism
   d. Animalizing

6. These animals were considered sacred by several early civilizations and the Egyptian culture worshipped it through the goddess Nut.
   a. Horse
   b. Cow
   c. Sheep
   d. Pig

7. Shaman would each have an animal _____ who was their guide in the spirit world.
   a. Pet
   b. Familiar
   c. Ancestor
   d. Agonist

15 Animals in Mythology, Art, Literature, and Screen

Objectives

○ To summarize the various animals used symbolically in Greek mythology

○ To examine animals in other historical uses related to mythology

○ To learn about Celtic and Nordic myths

○ To learn about Aesop's Fables

○ To learn about some American myths and beliefs related to animals

Greek mythology

- Animals played a vivid part of the writings of the early Greeks
- Both domestic and wild animals were part of the stories portrayed through poetry and prose
- In fact, over 150 wild animals are mentioned in the writings over the centuries between the times of the Greek writers Anyte and Agathias

Mammals

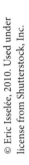

© Eric Isselée, 2010. Used under license from Shutterstock, Inc.

- *Lions* were common animals found in the lore of the ancient Greek writers.

  - *The king of beasts was slain with lances + spears by the heros of their stories.*

- An early poem told of a priest from the sect of the goddess Cybele finding shelter in a cave during a severe snow storm. He found he was sharing his abode with a lion. To scare the beast away, he beat a kettle drum used in the rituals to his goddess.

- The lives of many lion-slayers are also chronicled, including the god-man Hercules who slays a Nemean lion.

As a result of the portrayal of lions as the king of beasts, many brave men had lions sculpted onto their tombs.

Other cats

- Leopards and lynx are also mentioned in many of the Greek stories.
- For example, in a poem to Eros by the writer Meleager, the writer refuses the "god of love" a dwelling place near his heart, because to do so would be like "keeping a lynx beside goats."

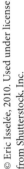

© Eric Isselée, 2010. Used under license from Shutterstock, Inc.

Domestic cats

- Rarely referred to, as in early Greece, most "mousing" was done by tame ferrets or weasels
- One cat story is of a partridge (not in a pear tree) who becomes the pet of Agathias Scholasticus. A stray cat bites the partridge's head off, and Agathias swears he will solemnly slaughter the murderer over the corpse of its victim
- More about cats (not necessarily Greek)

- Ancient Egypt
  - The cat was sacred to the cat-headed goddess Bast and to kill one was punishable by death
  - If a cat died, its owner went into mourning, shaving his eyebrows and performing elaborate funeral rites
  - Cat cemeteries were established on the banks of the Nile, the cats were mummified and laid to rest
  - The chariot of Freyja, the Scandinavian fertility goddess, was drawn by cats

- The reference to cats was not due to its mousing ability, but to the beauty of its eyes which were strangely reminiscent of the moon.

- In the East, the cat is said to bear away the souls of the dead
- In West Africa, the natives accept that the human soul passes into the body of a cat at death
- However, Christian Europe reduced the status of the cat from sacred to devil

Witchcraft and cats

- It was generally assumed that a witch could take the shape of a cat only nine times, because of the belief that cats had nine lives

  - Cats were most often a witch's familiar.

Vampire cats?

- Were common in Japan, but were easily recognizable because they had two tails

- One superstition is that cats crept into the cradle to suck the breath from young babies.

Prophetic sneezes

- A single sneeze, near a bride on her wedding morning, will forecast a happy marriage, but on other occasions it might portend rain

  - 3 sneezes in succession were a warning that the whole household would catch a cold soon.

United States

- Cat was a devil, a witch or a witch's imp, but at the same time its whiskers were often used to conjure magic and charms
- Southern belief also says if you kick a cat you will get rheumatism

- If you drown a cat, the devil will get you

- Yet a broth made from boiling a black cat was believed to cure consumption.

Bears

- Mentioned rarely in the anthologies
- However, a bear hunter is chronologized by Didot, while Homer makes a single reference to bears in his works.

- The most likely reason is that bears were rare in the Anthology regions of the world.

Wolves

- Were a popular animal subject with the Greek authors
- Theocritus wrote a poem consoling Thyrsis for the loss of a kid goat
- Another story tells of a shipwrecked mariner who swims to shore, only to be slain by a wolf as he sets foot on land
- An Egyptian "tail" (tale) describes an account of a pack of wolves forming a wolf chain by holding onto each other's tails to form a bridge across the Nile to pursue a traveler

Other stories

- Wolf-hounds slaying Euripides and sheep catching a wolf
- Diphilus, an early comic poet, calls the inhabitants of Argos wolves
- Lucilius accuses Gamus of having the appetite of five wolves
- Werewolves were made famous in the tales of Arcadia

Deer

- Often mentioned in Greek writings, as they heavily populated Erymanthus and the Arcadian forest region of Maenalus (a favored spot of Apollo and Pan)
- One famous statue of Hercules contains an epigram of his killing of the Maenalian hind
- According to the early poets, such as Xenophon, deer were hunted with hounds and killed with spears and arrows, or were driven into nets

- Antlers were considered trophies and were hung on trees.

Wild boars

- Were common in the Greek isles and were known for their savagery + reckless bravery.
- A special breed of hounds, described by Philippus, was employed against them because the ordinary sheep-dogs were usually killed during boar fights

- And more boars…
- While boars were usually villains, one story tells of a boar sinking its tusks into a ram which was about to gore a child with its twisted horns
- Boars were sacrificed to Artemis the huntress
- And the famous boar-hunters Polyaenus and Xenophilus dedicated trophies of their chase to their gods

Bulls

- Were a popular topic, such as the *urus* of Caesar
- The emperor Hadrian, wrote that Trajan offered a gold-encrusted bull horn to Zeus as part of his booty from the Getae in Hungary
- Addaeus tells of a brave man who kills a vicious bull by driving his spear through the bulls temple
- European bison
  ○ On the other hand, bison are described as having stubby horns
  ○ Both bulls and bison were often requested at beast fights
  ○ One story tells of the death of a toreador who, after killing many wild bulls in the stadium, falls victim to one himself.

© andrewshka, 2010. Used under license from Shutterstock, Inc.

Donkeys

- The first unicorns?
- One tale tells of a Scythian ass whose marvelous horn, A godlike ornament was dedicated to Paian by Alexander of Macedon.

The old writings often mention this beast. Some describe a horselike creature, called a monoceros that had fantastic moral and physical attributes.

However, other writers described what may have been a rhinoceros.

© Nessi, 2010. Used under license from Shutterstock, Inc.

Many other mammals

- Hares, mice, rats, hedgehogs, monkeys, bats
- Lucilius makes fun of a woman called Bito who has a very large nose and who is very unchaste–he calls her a monkey
- Another story tells of a woman who marries a hairy ape and produces a brood of ape-men

Birds

Eagles are the most common birds found in the literature, as they were the creatures of Zeus and the only bird to dwell with him in the heavens.

* They served as an emblem of bravery, similar to the lion.

* One was sculpted on Plato's tomb to represent the "aspiring element of his soul that gazed into the starry home of the gods."
* And…
* There are many stories about Zeus's justice in relation to eagles.
* One tells of an eagle that, when pierced by a Cretan archer, fell upon the man and hit with such a force that the archer was killed as well

© Vallentin Vassileff, 2010. Used under license from Shutterstock, Inc.

Ravens and crows

* The next most common birds found in Greek literature.

* The belief that the cawing of crows portends rain was first expressed by early greek writers.

* Crows live very long lives according to the early writers, and thus many jokes were made about old people living to "thrice a crow's age."
* Aristotle wrote about white crows. The story was that crows were originally all white, but were changed to black by Apollo because he was annoyed with one bird who brought him unsatisfactory news about a girl he had fallen for.

Reptiles

* Fourteen different reptiles are mentioned in Greek anthology.

Snakes of the adder and viper families are most often the culprits in stories, biting and killing both man and other beasts.

* The asp's bite was often compared to the pain of rejected love.

Dragons

* Often treated in Greek literature as synonymous with a certain type of snake called *ophis*.
* Most dragons mentioned seemed to be nothing more than mere snakes; however, a fragment of a story from Nestor of Laranda describes how a thirsty dragon engulfed the whole Kephisus brook to the disgust of the nymphs who lived there.

- Lysander is warned in a Delphic oracle about another dragon.
- "Beware the dragon, treacherous son of earth, coming up from behind."

Crocodiles

- Often alluded to, and credited with a sense of justice, but not for their hypocritical tears!
- Archelaus, an Egyptian, told a story of a dead crocodile who metamorphosed into a mass of scorpions

Chameleons

- *Also prominently mentioned for their colorful and changing skin tones*

- Apollo was the lord and destroyer of locus and other vermin, and was also a killer of lizards, and is so depicted in a statue slaying a lizard. The statue was housed in Rome and later at the Louvre.
- A spotted lizard called *galeotes* was used in divination practices and was also associated with worship of Apollo.

Sea beasts

- Mention of sea creatures is fairly rare in the anthology.

- *Fish are rarely mentioned (perhaps because to write an ode to a dead herring would not be romantic!)*

- Talk of sea serpents is very rare, with only one mention by Gaetulicus of a sea beast devouring a drowning man

Dolphin

- *The ancients classified the dolphin half-way between a mammal and a fish, but usually spoke of it as a fish.*

- There are many accounts of these marine mammals in the ancient writings.
- Bianor recounts the story of Arion who is thrown overboard by a hoard of pirates, but is rescued by a dolphin. In the story, the author marvels that the sea could contain beasts that are more just than man. Later, a marble statue was made to commemorate this story.

Insects and creeping things

Insects and the like are the most mentioned members of the animal kingdom in the anthology and other ancient writings.

- The species mentioned include the ant, spider, scorpion, wasp, beetle, worms, leech, bees, crickets, cicada, locusts, fly, gnat, mosquito, tick, flea, louse, and bug.

- Lucilius describes Menestratus astride upon an ant as if it were an elephant, and another little man is described as seated on a flying ant, similar to Pegasus.
- The art and cleverness of spiders to weave is often praised

Wasps

- Was regarded as a symbol of malignancy and cruel people are compared to them and their sting
- According to Archelaus, this insect *originated by flying out the dead body of a horse.*

Worms and maggots

- *were most naturally associated with the dead*

- In one sepulchral epigram, the use of maggots that drop from the head of goats is described.
- Herodicus wrote about thorn-worms who browsed on thorny passages in books, thus came the saying "bookworm"

Animal literature

- Demetrius of Phaeton introduced a new form of animal literature in 300 BC which moved the Greeks away from the mythological stories into a more realistic and moralistic vantage.
- These animal tales were considered suitable for children and were often used in teaching in the boys schools of antiquity.
- These fables were much less mythological than the epics of Homer and gave good moral teaching to young people—both in ancient times and even for today's young people.

- *The essence of these tales portrays the wise and grateful animal vs. a vile animal trickster.*

Aesop's Fables

- According to the Life of Aesop, he was a Samoan slave who was famous for his wise counsel and witty pranks and sayings. His sayings were quoted by many including Aristotle who used Aesop's story of the fox and hedgehog. According to Aristotle, the story was used to illustrate the counsel for the defense of a politician charged with corruption

Celtic and Nordic mythology

- Lore and myths related to animals were passed down from generation to generation of Celts in tales told around campfires.
- During the early Christian period, these tales were compiled in written form.
- Irish prose tales regarding animals are found in three major groups and include the *Book of Invasions*, the *Fionn Cycle*, which relates the story of the hero Finn, and from the Ulster Cycle, a book called *The Cattle Raid of Cooley.*
- Wales has a similar group of ancient writings which tell the legends of gods and heroes, and the supernatural world, including enchanted beasts.

- A major thread in the Welsh stories is the ability to morph.

- Similar myths in Nordic traditions. Magic beasts continually interrelate w/ human heros luring them to the other world.

- Some animals, especially pigs, have the ability to self-regenerate, being constantly killed, eaten, and reborn to go through the cycle again to supply the Otherworld Feast with meat

Hunting and wild animals

- A close relation between the hunter and hunted is described and connected to the divine world.
- Hunted animals were perceived as messengers of Otherworld powers and could bring humans to the underworld.

- The hunted animal could possess magical characteristics + could transform into human or zoomorphic forms

- Tales consisted of boars + stags.

- These beasts would lead the hunters to secluded places where they encountered supernatural beings and had perilous experiences.
- In Welsh literature, the stag is the means whereby the hero Pwyll encounters the leader of the underworld.
- While the stag is not supernatural, it serves as the link between the world of humans and the gods.

Stags

associated w/ speed, strength, + wisdom. Sometimes they could be supernatural

- For example, in the *Tale of Culhwch and Olwen*, a supernatural stag speaks with some of King Arthur's men and helps in the quest for Mabon.
- In the Fionn Cycle, Finn's wife Sava is part-deer and part-woman. The first time Finn meets her, she in the shape of a fawn, having been transformed by the magic of the Black Druid. Her son, Oisin, has a strong affinity

for deer and is described as half-fawn, and half-child. His name, in fact means "Little Deer."

- In the Irish traditions, stags are associated with the divine world.
- The Irish goddess Flidhais, deity of forests and wild things, kept deer like herds of cattle.
- Stags could change shape.
- In one story, some young men who are in trouble with their lord uncle are changed into deer.

Boars and pigs

- Very important (in real life) to the early peoples of Ireland and Wales.
- They were used as a primary source of meat, and also played an important role in their religion.

*Fierce wild boars w/ supernatural powers are often mentioned

Birds

- Were perceived as symbolic and magical creatures due to their ability to fly and sing.
- They were seen as messengers between man and the other world and could serve as mediators between god and man.
- In the "Irish Happy Otherworld," magical birds could sing sick or wounded men to sleep and then heal them with their supernatural powers.
- One story describes a goddess who has a flock of birds on an island.

— The birds are similiar to ravens, but have green heads (grackles?) and they lay eggs of blue and crimson. If a human eats one, they'll grow feathers

[feathers come off in the bath]

Domestic Animals

Cattle

- were symbol of prosperity
- The most famous of the cattle stories tells of two supernatural bulls and their vicious fight.
- The fight actually depicts the real-life struggle between two warring tribes.
- The bulls are very large and have human intelligence.
- The bulls are actually "skin-changers," men who have metamorphosed from human shape.
- Bulls also played a role in the selection of Irish kings.
- A bull is killed in a ritual and a man is selected to eat the meat and drink the broth made from the bull's flesh. The man then goes to sleep and dreams who the next ruler is to be

Dogs

- *Had very close association to man and were highly valued members of the family.*
- Dog rituals were also held, where dogs were assigned a role in the underworld.
- Many tales are found regarding supernatural dogs, such as the underworld lords shining white dogs with red ears.
- The hounds of Annwn, the underworld lord, were death omens.
  ◦ These animals were described as small, speckled, and greyish-red, chained, and led by a black, horned figure.
  ◦ These ghost dogs only appeared at night to foretell death, sent from Annwn to seek corpses and human souls.
- Sirius, the dog star *•Venerated by the people of the Nile*

  — Depended on the rise and fall of the great river for their livelihood.
- When time for flood drew near, they watched for the rise of Sirius (the brightest star in the sky)
- They worshipped Sirius, who was a faithful dog and never failed them

© Eric Isselée, 2010. Used under license from Shutterstock, Inc.

Horses

- Also had a special relationship with the Celts
- They were vital in battle and in successful hunting
- Horses were used in gift exchanges between man and the underworld
- Horses and kings

— Giraldus Cambrensis chronicles an Irish tradition regarding the inauguration of kings. A white mare is sacrificed and her meat cooked in a cauldron. The king-elect must sit in the cauldron + bathe in the juices + feed on the flesh + broth.

Enchantment and shape changing

- Beasts in the Celtic myths are often given supernatural powers and many can change shapes, skin-turn, or morph from their form to that of a human or other animal
- The Salmon of Wisdom, who appears in both Welsh and Irish myths, is one such fantastic beast.
  ◦ He is consulted by Culhwch and Arthur.
  ◦ According to legend, Finn is given the salmon by a fisherman to cook, but is told to not eat the meat.
  ◦ However, he burns his finger while cooking the fish and tastes the flesh.

© patrimonio designs limited, 2010. Used under license from Shutterstock, Inc.

- ○ When he does so, he begins to gain greater knowledge, so he eats the whole fish and becomes very wise (remind you of Adam in the Garden of Eden?)
- Morphing occurs in one of three ways in Celtic tradition

• a god / superhuman changes from human animal

1. The shape changing can be imposed on another as punishment / revenge.

2. Creature is transformed for a particular purpose.

Frogs
3. by choice.

- Does not appear often in mythology, but when it does, it is with either extreme repulsion or respect
- Associated with rain in India and South America
- A tribe in Venezuela kept frogs and beat them in times of drought
- Chinese tales say the dew brings frog spawn down from the moon and the frog is called the "celestial chicken"
- Shan and Karen tribes of Burma regard the frog as the enemy of the moon, the demon that swallows it at eclipses.

In Europe

- Frog is an ingredient of magic
- Highly regarded in the "medical" half-world between magic and science
- Toads were preferred to frogs in witchcraft
- In some areas frogs were always killed on sight because they were thought to be witches.

In United States and other countries

- It is deadly bad luck to kill a frog; it would at least make your cow's milk bloody
- Here a frog is positive magic; lucky if it enters the house or if you dream of frogs
- You make a wish on the first frog heard in the spring

- Gamblers will be winners if they meet a frog in the road on their way to gamble.

- American superstition: a hood-shaped bone of the frog will act as a love charm if placed among the clothing of the person whose love in being sought

Frog's medicinal powers

- Pliny the Elder discusses the "magic"
  - ○ It was carried around a cornfield and buried in the center before sowing, and dug up before harvest

- Hung up in orchards and vineyards to protect from fog and storms and in a granary to preserve the grain

  - A person found to be suffering from acugte eye inflammation could be cured by hanging the corresponding eye of a frog around his neck.

- Galen— If you hold a frog boiled in H_2O + vinegar in your mouth for some time, it is quite good for a toothache

- Marcellus— A toothace could be cured by spiting into a frog's mouth and asking it to take the pain away.

- Arabic text of ninth century
  - Recalls an ancient belief that a woman who spit into a frog's mouth would not conceive for a year
- Slav tribe
  - Frogs brought children, not storks
- Frogs were used in medicine until the seventeenth century
  - Sufferers from epilepsy were said to have been cured by a powder made from frog's liver
  - Eye of a frog plucked before sunrise and swallowed, or worn as an amulet, was a remedy for fever
- American: A soup made from 9 frogs will cure whooping cough.

- To cure a headache, you must bind a live frog to your head and keep it there until it dies

Study Questions

1. The most common animals to be found in the lore of the ancient Greek writers that were slain with lances and spears were
   a. Lions
   b. Tigers
   c. Bears
   d. Oh my!

2. Domestic cats were rarely mentioned by the early Greeks, as most of the mousing was done by
   a. Ferrets and weasels
   b. Meerkats
   c. Lynx
   d. Mongoose and rabbits

3. There is a Greek story about a shipwrecked mariner who swims to shore, but is slain by a
   a. Bear
   b. Lion
   c. Wolf
   d. Boar

4. What animals were common in the Greek isles and were known for their savagery and reckless bravery?
   a. Wolves
   b. Bears
   c. Lions
   d. Wild boars

5. Which of our modern day rodeo events may have come from ancient Greece?
   a. Team roping
   b. Calf roping
   c. Steer wrestling
   d. Bull riding

6. Another name that was given to unicorn-like animals was
   a. Monoceros
   b. Dinoceros
   c. Trinoceros
   d. Quadnoceros

7. If you wanted to insult someone and say they were unchaste, you could call them a
   a. Pig
   b. Hedgehog
   c. Bat
   d. Monkey

8. These animals were associated with speed, strength, and wisdom. Sometimes they could be supernatural.
   a. Stags
   b. Boars
   c. Pigs
   d. Birds

9. What animals were considered a symbol of prosperity?
   a. Dogs
   b. Pigs
   c. Birds
   d. Cattle

16 History of How Animal Ethics Developed

Objectives

○ To understand the stages of the ways humans ethically thought about animals

○ To learn about the ancient philosophers perspectives on animal ethics

○ To learn how the SPCA got started

○ To learn about the other "ethical" animal organizations

What we already know...

- Hunter (gatherer)
- Animals were perceived as rational, intelligent beings with spirits/souls
- Therefore, hunted animals were treated with respect
- These respectful beliefs date back to pre-historic times because of the number of carnivores that could prey upon the stone-age humans (sabre-tooth cat, bears, etc.)

- 11,000 years ago
- Agriculture and animal husbandry began...

> - Animal garden spirits claimed the status "zoomorphic gods"
> - Some gods attained animal form
> - Egyptian book of the dead prohibited mistreatment of animals

- We know some gods attained animal form
- Egyptian *Book of the Dead* prohibited mistreatment of animals
- Even though ancient Egyptians ate animals, humans were still expected to treat all creatures with respect and kindness
- And....
- We already established that cattle (bulls) reflected power and fertility
- As time went on, this respect for animals was lost
- Gods became associated more with the agriculture cycle and animal sacrifice was used to please them

> - Essentially religious systems took over
>
> - However, this change in relationships was a slow moving process.

As we move on in history
- Intermittent history of vegetarianism
- Veggie communities may have existed 8,000 years ago; especially among priests
- Example: Greek poet Hesiod of the Golden Age

Pythagoras (sixth century BCE)

- Both mathematical genius and mystic

> - Taught that there is a transmigration of souls between animals and humans.

- Based his vegetarianism on religious belief as well as health and ethical concerns (confirmed the case for animals)

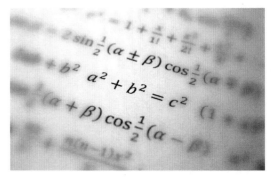

- However, some disagree as to the degree of vegetarianism that he upheld

Socrates (470–399 BCE)

- Indifferent to what he ate

Plato (428–347 BCE)

- Was influenced by Pythagoras and believed that philosophers should be vegetarians
- However, he did not condem hunting, butchering or raising livestock for consumption.

Aristotle

- As we know, he was opposed to vegetarianism
- Affirmed that animals do possess souls; but animals lacked reason therefore have no moral status.

Augustine and Thomas Aquinas

- We have also already learned that these two church fathers followed the veins of Aristotle
- Aquinas actually taught that the life of animals is preserved for man

First century AD

- Most philosophers believed that animals were not of our moral community because they lacked reason

- Although a few Romans were still advocating Vegetarianism, most Romans did not.

- And does that surprise us????

Plutarch

- Greek priest at Delphi 45–125 AD

© Jozef Sedmak, 2010. Used under license from Shutterstock, Inc.

- May have been the first to preach vegetarianism for benevolence sake, not because of the transmigration of souls
- He exhibited a love of animals, but not at the expense of humans.

Medieval Times

- Ambivalence toward animals that were taken for granted
- Many stories of interactions between saints and animals

Sixteenth and seventeenth centuries

- Great social change
- Emphasized the boundaries between man and animal
- They believed all things were created for the benefit and pleasure of "man"
- Cruel medieval practices such as bear-baiting, bull-baiting, persecution of cats, etc. continued and was joined by the dissection of living animals for scientific purposes

- We spoke of Leonardo da Vince already (who was a vegetarian as well!)

"Beasts"

Despite compassion for animals in the seventeenth century, the most common view was that "beasts" had an inferior kind of reason.

- included sensibility, imagination, memory; but no power of reflection

Main dispute (which we have already looked at...)

- Those who held that all humanity had dominion over the creatures V. S.
- Those who believed that this dominion should be confined to a privileged group of humans
- Example: slavery was attacked because people were being treated like animals, but slavery of animals was taken for granted

At the same time (still sixteenth and seventeenth centuries)

- Pets are becoming more popular
  - Monkeys, tortoises, otters, rabbits, squirrels, hares, mice, hedgehogs, bats and toads, birds

- The spread of pet-keeping created the psychological foundation for the view that some animals were entitled to moral consideration.

End of seventeenth century

- Anthropocentrism (human centered)
  - Anthropocentrism was still the prevailing outlook, but by the eighteenth century, non-anthropocentric sensibilities became much more widely dispersed and were more explicitly supported by the religious and philosophical teaching of the time (*The Animal Ethics Reader*, 2nd edition, Armstrong and Botzler).
- Cruelty to animals was regularly denounced

  "moral awakening."

- This campaign was enhanced by moral status

Vegetarian movement

- Once the belief that animals had feelings and should be treated with kindness was accepted, in the eyes of some, it became repugnant to kill them for meat
- From about 1790 forward, there was an increase in the vegetarian movement

  – Many people did not want to kill animals for food and slaughterhouses were hidden.

Later in the eighteenth century...

- It was decided that animals could think and reason in an inferior way

  – This lead to a growing belief that humans were animals that managed to better themselves.

- Germany and Britain courts
  - Punished cruelty to animals

  – Animals themselves had no rights, but maltreatment of them violated the direct duty to God.

Martin's Act, 1822

• First national law against cruelty to animals

- "An offense to wantonly beat, abuse or ill-treat any horse, donkey, sheep, cow or other cattle (unless it was property of the offender)"
- Did not include bulls
- The fine was no more than 5 pounds and no less than 10 schillings

Organized animal welfare

- An organized animal welfare movement emerged
  - What helped this was the Industrial Revolution which reduced the dependence on animals.

1824

- Member of Parliament and churchmen

Two committees:

1. to publish literature to influence public opinion

2. to adopt measures for ~~inspecting~~ inspecting the treatment of animals

- SPCA (Society for the Prevention of Cruelty to Animals)
  ○ 150 prosecutions for cruelty
  ○ Campaigns against bull-baiting, dog-fighting, horse and cattle abuse
  ○ Condemned painful experiments on animals
  ○ 1840, Queen gave it "royal" distinction (RSPCA)

Victorian Era

- Greatest campaign of Victorian Era
- Britain was against use of live animals in experiments
- 1876, Cruelty to Animals Act
  — A license was required along with certificate from the government.

Women of the time

- Very prominent anti-vivisectionists
- However women were viewed by scientists as infantile, animal-like, and belonging to nature instead of civilization

- Anyone who opposed animal research was considered irrational, sentimental and "womanly"

1890s

- Medical profession is gaining power due to success with experiments in medical microbiology
  ○ Because of this, plus other happenings
  ○ "the anti-vivisection movement ceased to be a vital and mass movement after the turn of the century"

(*The Animal Ethics Reader*, 2nd edition, Armstrong and Botzler)

U.S. concerns

- Derived from British precedent
- 1641, Massachusetts Bay colony
- Approved laws protecting animals

- But orginizations were not formed until 1866

1866 ASPCA

American Society for the Prevention of Cruelty to Animals

- Founder Henry Bergh

  - Known for defending overworked and abused carriage horses in NY

  ◌ Successfully prosecuted many people for cruel treatment of livestock, cock-fighting, and dog-fighting
- George Angell
  ◌ Founded the Massachusetts SPCA

  - Emphasized human education

- More statewide SPCAs were established

Anti-vivisection

- American anti-vivisection movement was unsuccessful
- Speculated that the pioneering spirit of the American may have welcomed science more easily

Vegetarianism

- Adapted by some in United States and Britain
- Word was coined in 1847

"vegetare" Latin for "to grow"

After World War I

- Animal welfare movement lost mass appeal
- Probably because meat during times of disease and war can save lives
- Welfare organizations declined into charities

1929 and after

- National Antivivisection Society formed
- Nothing happened until 1950s when the Animal Welfare Institute and Humane Society began

1955

- Humane Slaughter Act

1959

Wild Horses Act
- Also founded International Society for Animal Rights and Fund for Animals

© mariait, 2010. Used under license from Shutterstock, Inc.

Post-World War II

- Saw little improvement in animal conditions
  - ○ Could have been because political parties were very conservative
- However, in the 1960s in Britain, human concern moved into animal rights movement

Justice and fairness in our treatment of animals.

Hunt Saboteurs in 1963

- Formation of this group:
  - ○ "Appears to be the first organization to speak openly and uncompromisingly of members a proponents of rights of animal in the modern sense" (Finsen and Finsen, 1994).

-Tactics involved direct action

- Ruth Harrison published *Animal Machines*
  - ○ In which the term "factory farming" was first used
  - ○ Closed doors

1970s and 1980s

- Increase in legal and illegal actions of animal rights groups
- ALF (Animal Liberation Front)
  - ○ England, 1972

  -Led raids on animal labs, factory farms

- When Margaret Thatcher became prime minister, Britain began to punish these groups and illegal activities decreased

1990s

- British-led European movement began again
- Prime Minister John Major invited animal welfarists to Downing St.
- In United States
  - ○ PETA (People for the Ethical Treatment of Animals)
  - ○ Trans-Species Unlimited
  - ○ Farm Animal Reform Movement
  - ○ Mobilization for Animals
  - ○ In Defense of Animals
- Target of most of these→ *Animals in labs*

© Eric Isselée, 2010. Used under license from Shutterstock, Inc.

ALF

- U.S. ALF organizations
- Property damage
- Have placed people in danger
- Burnt private homes of researchers
- Did extensive damage to the ~~United States~~ in the 1990s

  U of A

Late 1990s

- Disputes between those supporting animal rights and those supporting animal welfare
- These disputes have taken some of the force out of the rights movements in United States

Overall...

- The U.S. animal welfare movement is a collection of national and local organizations and has not been very effective
- More recently
  - ○ Animals Voice
  - ○ Institute for Animals and Society

    – Both of these have once again raised ethical issues

The final summary...

- In general, animal ethics is a subject marked with ambivalence
- It all comes down to the basis of the moral value or moral status of animals
- A status that will <u>NEVER</u> be agreed upon by all people

Study Questions

1. This mathematical genius and mystic taught that there is a transmigration of souls between animals and humans.
   a. Pythagoras
   b. Aristotle
   c. Hesiod
   d. Socrates

2. Who may have been the first to preach vegetarianism for benevolence sake, not because of transmigration of souls?
   a. Pythagoras
   b. Plutarch
   c. Plato
   d. Aristotle

3. Anthropocentrism means
   a. Animal-centered
   b. Human-centered
   c. Pro-vivisection
   d. Anti-vivisection

4. In 1822, what was the first National law against cruelty to animals?
   a. Martin's Act
   b. Animal Welfare Act
   c. Royal Act
   d. Victorian Act

5. Which animal group originated in Britain but used illegal actions to promote animal rights?
   a. PETA
   b. ALF
   c. BARK
   d. WOOF

17 Experimenting with Humans and Animals: A Brief History

Objectives

○ To learn about the two opinions of animal experimentation

○ To learn about some of the first philosophers and scientists to experiment with animals and humans

○ To understand how the church and government was involved in this area

○ To see what new developments helped in these areas of research

○ To learn about the federal laws and regulations controlling animal research

○ To examine a few examples of how animal research has benefitted both human and animal medicine

Herophilus in Alexandria

- Greek physician (330–260 BC)
- Along with this colleague Erasistratus,
- *Given permission to cut into a living man*

  —Not to cure, but to look

- condemned criminal scheduled for execution

Two opinions of this:

Empirics

—Strongly opposed to dissection of any kind

- Relied on observation of the patient
- Claimed philosophy and experimentation were irrelevant to medical practice

Hippocrates supported this opinion

- The physician could gain knowledge of disease only through repeated observation
- Said vivisection (cutting open) gave knowledge of the dead, not the living
- Subject usually died anyway

Dogmatists

- Celsus, Herophilus, Erasistratus
- *Believed that knowledge of anatomy was critical to medical practice*

- They dissected to learn more about the body's internal workings because mere observation of the exterior was not enough
- Followed the model of Aristotle

Aristotle

- Had very limited access to the human body
- Taboos and because of the inherent risk of infection and shock
- Therefore… *Dissection and experimentation on animals was a necessary alternative to research on humans.*

- Dissected many dead animals; experimented on live animals
- Assumed an analogy existed between human and animal
- Never considered dissecting a human

- Believed that only humans had intelligence and therefore rational souls
- Animal souls possessed emotion but not reason
- Humans and animals did not occupy the same moral plane

  — No such thing as justice or injustice to animals

Celsus

- Pointed out that deliberate vivisection gave more valuable information than chance wound observation

  — He argued that the sacrifice of a few for the many was justified.

- He lived and wrote in ancient Rome, where a criminal could "pay" for his crime by making his body useful to the community

Herophilus

— First to distinguish nerves from the other tissues

- Established the brain, not heart, as the center of the nervous system
- His descriptions of the human brain far surpassed Aristotle's
- He named the retina, as well as some other parts

After Herophilus and Erasistratus…

Galen

- Physician to Emperor Marcus Aurelius (175 AD)
- Along with Hippocrates, the most important physician in antiquity

- His ideas dominated Western thought until the Renaissance
- One of the greatest anatomists and experimenters in antiquity
- Never dissected a human; only used animals
- Advised his students to cut "without pity or compassion" into a living animal
- Had little concern for the animals and by our standards, he was very cruel
- But he lived in a world of cruelty and violence in which gladiatorial combat was as common as football
- Animals were killed for amusement
- One form of public execution was to throw condemned humans together with wild animals for entertainment

Augustine (354–430)

The most influential of the early ~~test~~ church fathers

- Acknowledged the chain of being in his definition of human dominion

© RoJo Images, 2010. Used under license from Shutterstock, Inc.

Middle Ages

St. Francis of Assisi and St. Thomas Aquinas

- Revisited Augustine's doctrines in sixteenth and seventeenth centuries
- They also revived the techniques of Galen and the Alexandrians
- Francis reintroduced the works of Aristotle and some of Galen to Western Europe

  — In this period, anatomical studies began to resume in some Italian schools of medicine and dead animals were used.

Sixteenth Century

Dr. William Harvey

- Performed experiments on animals to disprove Galen (who said arteries contained blood not air and that it moved back and forth in a section)
- Harvey said blood circulated throughout the whole body and the heart was responsible for this

  — Harvey went on to explain many facets of the circulatory system

More facts…

- More animal research (both living and dead) occurred because use of humans in sixteenth century was still unacceptable
- Local governments granted the use of executed criminals for public dissections
- Leonardo da Vinci described dissections and vivisections he witnessed and performed.

- Grave robbing became illegal
- When did moral concern begin?
- Galen wasted no thought on moral consideration when he cut open living animals
- He was a man of his time
- But by the 1530s, when Vesalius duplicated some of Galen's experiments, social standards had changed

Vesalius

- Used the public anatomy spectacle to have a moral impact on its audience
- Viewing the end of all flesh reminded the audience of the importance of their souls
- The suffering of the animals induced compassion

- In the finale of his public anatomy, he vivisected a pregnant animal, expertly manipulating both the animals and his audience.

Seventeenth century

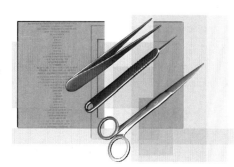

Use of animals in experiments increased
- Popular attitudes toward animals also began to change
- Around 1800 public anatomy disappeared
- Animal sports (except hunting) were for lower class people
- Pet keeping increased
- In 1824, First animal protection society was founded in London
  SPCA: Society for the protection of the Creulty to animals

1846

- Introduction of anesthesia (ether)
- Laudanum (liquid opium)
- Alcohol
- Early in the nineteenth century
  - Isolated morphine from the opium
  - Pain reliever

So what about now? How do we define animal rights and welfare?

Merriam-Webster's definition…

- Rights (as to fair and humane treatment) regarded as belonging fundamentally to all animals

Thefreedictionary.com definition

- The rights to humane treatment claimed on behalf of animals, especially the right not to be exploited for human purposes

Animal rights

- Bring varied visions to many people
- A sounding cry from the heart, born of deep-rooted love for all creatures of this earth
- A call to arms to raise protest against what they consider wrongs by society against the helpless
- A picture of people who have nothing better to do than to try to stop a sport others enjoy
- To some, the words invoke fear of loss of property, bodily injury, or even loss of life

However...

- To many people animal rights simply invoke memories of people they don't understand, who carry banners with disturbing pictures and slogans berating research, eating meat, or opposing circuses or rodeos

For over a hundred years...

- Philosophers, scientists, politicians, students, teachers, etc. have discussed and debated animal rights
- How do they obtain rights?
- Are they born with rights?
- Do we give them rights?
- What is an animal's legal standing?
- What if the difference, if any, between animal and man?

Unanswerable questions

These are all questions that cannot be answered by any one answer.

- People will always be debating these and other questions relating to animal rights
- Because of the controversial topic we are not going to dwell on the animal rights issue
- There are many groups and organizations that cover extremist attitudes to good practices

Therefore, we will concentrate on the animal welfare issue and what the government has done to ensure the welfare of animals.

Animal Welfare

We will talk about the laws and regulations affecting the use of animals in education, research and testing.

- The Animal Welfare Act
- Federal law (1966)

  Designed to prevent the theft of family dogs and cats; includes animals in research, exhibitions, and pets

- Covers vet care, cage sizes, housing, comfort, transport, anesthesia, analgesia, euthanasia, restricted survival surgeries; licenses dealers

- Definition excludes: farm animals, lab rodents, and birds
- Issue: Why not include lab rodents?
- Administered by USDA (United States Department of Agriculture)
  - Unannounced site visits/inspections at any time
  - Mandatory annual reporting of animal numbers
  - Noncompliance with law means no government funding until institution is in compliance
  - Establishes the Institutional Animal Care and Use Committee (IACUC) as institutional regulatory authority for AWA (Animal Welfare Association)

Definite Challenge

Animal rights organizations wanted rats and mice to be included under this umbrella of protection

Public Health Service Policy (PHS)

- Fed law applies to vertebrate animals used in PHS funded research:

© kontur-vid, 2010. Used under license from Shutterstock, Inc.

- National Institutes of Health (NIH), National Cancer Institute (NCI)
- Includes: farm animals, birds, lab rodents, fish, amphibians, reptiles, any other species.
- Issued: *Guide for the Care and Use of Lab Animals* which has become the primo guide for institutions with animal care programs
- Policy is concerned with people welfare as well as animal
- Occupational health program to protect humans against animal hazards
- No routine inspection; NIH inspects several institutions per year checking for compliance
- Major violations lead to loss of ALL PHS funding to institution
- Must have IACUC group

Association for Assessment and Accreditation for Laboratory Animal Care (AAALAC)

- Sets the GOLD STANDARD for animal care.

- Inspects institutions who do animal research and want accreditation
- AAALAC accreditation means the highest quality of animal care
- Increases researchers chances for obtaining research grants
- University of Arizona has AAALAC accreditation!!!

Good Laboratory Practice Act

- Very cumbersome.

- Anything to be sold on open market for health purposes (drugs, implants, drugs, pacemakers, etc.) must have one safety study which equates to about sixteen file boxes of raw data

IACUC

• Enforced AWA, PHS, AAALAC policies

- Review and approve all campus animal activities
- Inspect all animal housing at least two times a year
- Review IACUC program
- Ensure training of all animal researchers
- Ensure adequate veterinary care
- Ensure human occupational health program is in place in each laboratory
- Investigate _any_ complaints of improper animal care on campus
- People who want to use animals in research

Protocols
- Written description of project
- Once approved, must follow protocol
- If not, protocol may be suspended or must make amendments to protocol which must be approved

The Three R's of Using Animals in Research

Replacement
— Use non-animal models (in vitro), invertebrates, or lower species first.

Reduction
— Use the lowest # of animals possible (stat. sig.)

Refinement
— Reduce pain and distress as much as possible
— Include enrichment of the animals environment

~~Include enrichment of the animals environment~~

- Ninety percent of all animals used in research are rodents
- Less than 1 percent are dogs, cats, or non-human primates

Major Medical Advances
- Fourteenth and fifteenth century, it was considered wrong to study human body/cadaver; therefore, they studied animals

Small Pox

- Edward Jenner, a microbiologist, studied small pox which was rampant in Europe in the seventeenth and eighteenth centuries
- He found that milk maids were immune to small pox *because they had been exposed to cow pox lesions on ~~affected~~ udders. (infected)*

© Laurent Renault, 2010. Used under license from Shutterstock, Inc.

Rabies

- Louis Pasteur
- First protective vaccine "Pasteur treatment"
- Series of twenty-one injections into abdominal muscles to protect against rabies bite
- *Used sheep and rabbits to develop vaccine*
- *- Also developed first anthrax vaccine.*

Advances in Twentieth Century

World War II

- Hitler was anti-vivisectionist
- Prison camps of humans were used in research
- At end of World War II
- All world leaders got together to prosecute the Nazis in Helsinki (Nuremberg trials)
- Came out with the Helsinki Accord and the Nuremberg code
- Humans cannot be used in research unless human signs off on it
- The code said *that any and all human research must be based on animal research that is done first.*

Some contributions of animals to modern medicine

- Blowfly larvae secrete alantoin
  - Promotes healing of deep wound, decaying tissues, and osteomyelitis

© Bork, 2010. Used under license from Shutterstock, Inc.

- Blister beetle provides cantharidin
  - Used in treatment of disorders in the urogenital system

- Bloodsucking leeches contain hirudin
  - Valuable anticoagulant of human blood

- Bee venom
  - Counters arthritis

- Snake venoms from several species
  - Utilized as a nonaddictive painkiller
  - Offers promise for treatment of thrombotic disorders

- The jaceracea (a Brazilian snake) harbors material in venom for the drug captopril
  - Helps many of the 25 million Americans who suffer from high blood pressure and other hypertension problems
  - Especially those people who do not respond to more traditional therapies

- Malaysian pit viper venom
  - Used commonly as an anticoagulant to help prevent heart attacks

- Toads secrete skin substances with toxic chemical
  - Being tested

Other ways...

- Butterflies, wasps, mice, salamanders, toads, sea urchins, and fruit flies have helped us with our basic understanding of genetics and embryology in humans
  - Have supplied us with clues on how to tackle genetic defects such as Down's syndrome and sickle cell anemia
- Cheetahs
  - Because of their cardiorespiratory capabilities that allow them to accelerate to 70 km/hour in a few strides is able to sustain a sudden and severe oxygen debt. Hence, the cheetah could provide clues for a treatment of heart disease, blood pressure, and circulatory disorders in humans

- Hansen's disease
  - Also known as leprosy
  - Afflicts at least 15 million people in developing countries
  - Very recently, scientists have finally tracked down an animal that contracts leprosy: the armadillo
- AIDS
  - The green monkey of central Africa can be infected by the HIV virus, but is totally unaffected by it.
  - Therefore, it can be researched for a vaccine

- The black bear
  - Hibernates for five months during the winter and relies on hormonal adaptation
  - These adaptations are assisting scientists in developing a low-protein and low-fluid diet for humans suffering from kidney failure

These are but a few examples of how animals have helped in human disease. But remember, they also help the whole animal population as well.

Study Questions

1. There are two opinions of using humans and animals for experimentation. Which opinion is based on the belief that knowledge of anatomy is critical to medical practice and followed the model of Aristotle?
   a. Empirics
   b. Dogmatists
   c. Consequentialists
   d. Socratic

2. Who believed that only humans had intelligence and therefore rational souls? He also said animal souls possessed emotion but not reason.
   a. Herophilus
   b. Erisistratus
   c. Aristotle
   d. Celsus

3. Who performed experiments on animals to disprove Galen? He said that blood circulated throughout the whole body and the heart was responsible for this.
   a. Galen
   b. Vesalius
   c. Augustine
   d. Harvey

4. Who used the public anatomy spectacle to have a moral impact on its audience?
   a. Galen
   b. Vesalius
   c. Augustine
   d. Harvey

5. Which of the following is NOT one of the three R's of animal research?
   a. Replacement
   b. Replenishment
   c. Reduction
   d. Refinement

6. For what did Edward Jenner find the vaccine by observing milk maids?
   a. Rabies
   b. Leprosy
   c. Anthrax
   d. Small pox

7. What animal can we use to study the HIV and AIDS because they can be infected but not affected by the virus?
    a. Armadillo
    b. Black Bear
    c. Green Monkey
    d. Cheetah

8. This mathematical genius and mystic taught that there is a transmigration of souls between animals and humans.
    a. Pythagoras
    b. Aristotle
    c. Hesiod
    d. Socrates